IMPROVEMENT FOR YOUNG ATHLETES 2nd ed.

How to Sprint Faster in Your Sport in 30 Workouts

For athletes ages 9-19 in football, soccer, baseball, basketball, field hockey, lacrosse, rugby, and tennis

By

George Blough Dintiman, Ed.D., International Authority on Speed Improvement for Team Sports

Graphic design by R. A. Underwood - 812.234.8181
thewood@gte.net

Speed Improvement for Young Athletes

How to Sprint Faster in Your Sport in 30 Workouts

By Dr. George Blough Dintiman

Published by: National Association of Speed and Explosion

P.O. Box 1784, Kill Devil Hills, NC 27948. Tel.: (252) 441-1185

Fax: (252) 449-4125 e-mail: Naseinc@earthlink.net

ISBN: 0-938074-26-1

Printed in the United States of America

Library of Congress Cataloging card No. 2005928625

"In loving memory of our father, Paul D. Dintiman (1946-1998). You taught us to work hard, play hard, and enjoy every day. Your strong will and spirit will be with us forever." - Scott, Jennifer, and Brandon

Contents

INTRODUCTION: HOW TO IMPROVE SPEED FOR YOUR SPORT.....6

Chapter 1

A SERIES OF TESTS TO GET YOU STARTED: HOW TO FIND
YOUR STRENGTHS AND WEAKNESSES.... 12

Chapter 2

WARM-UP, STRETCHING AND COOL-DOWN: HOW TO
PROTECT AND PREPARE YOUR BODY FOR EACH WORKOUT...... 24

Chapter 3

IMPROVING STRIDE RATE: HOW TO TAKE FASTER
STEPS 36

Chapter 4

IMPROVING YOUR STRIDE LENGTH: HOW TO TAKE
LONGER STEPS 65

Chapter 5

IMPROVING ACCELERATION: HOW TO START AND REACH
MAXIMUM SPEED FASTER... 74

Chapter 6

IMPROVING SPRINTING TECHNIQUE: HOW TO DEVELOP
PROPER FORM 79

Chapter 7

IMPROVING SPEED ENDURANCE: HOW TO GET INTO
CONDITION TO SPRINT SHORT DISTANCES 91

Chapter 8

PUTTING IT ALL TOGETHER: THE 30-WORKOUT PROGRAM 94

USING YOUR TRAINING PROGRAMS IN THE CORRECT ORDER 94
YOUR 30-WORKOUT SCHEDULE 95

MICRO CYCLE 1: PRECONDITIONING & ACCLIMATION 99
MICRO CYCLE 2: SPEED - STRENGTH 105
MICRO CYCLE 3: SPEED - SPECIFIC 112
MICRO CYCLE 4: HIGH INTENSITY 116

TABLE 8.1: WEIGHT TRAINING FOR EARLY ADOLESCENTS 122
TABLE 8.2: WEIGHT TRAINING FOR LATE ADOLESCENTS & ADULTS 124
TABLE 8.3: SPRINT ASSISTED TRAINING 130
TABLE 8.4: SPEED ENDURANCE TRAINING 133
TABLE 8.5: PLYOMETRICS 136
TABLE 8.6: SPRINT LOADING 138

Apendix 140
  A: YOUR TEST SCORE SHEETS 140
  B: SPEED EMPHASIS AREAS 144
  C: ABDOMINAL EXERCISES 146

Suggested Reading 148

INTRODUCTION:

HOW TO IMPROVE SPEED
FOR YOUR SPORT

Every athlete can improve their sprinting speed. Although it is true that heredity is important, keep in mind that "heredity only deals the cards; environment and training plays the hand." What this means is that regardless of your genetic make-up, you can get faster with proper training. On the other hand, even genetically gifted athletes will not reach their potential unless they follow a complete speed improvement program. The trick is to start the right training at the right time. If you are between the ages of 9-19 or older, you can safely begin a program that will make you faster and quicker by following the simple instructions and the 30 workouts in this book. The 30-workout program provides you with a total attack plan to improve acceleration and sprinting speed for your sport.

There are only five ways to improve your speed:

1. *Increase the number of steps you take per second.* This book shows you exactly how to train to increase your stride rate (steps per second) without shortening the length of your stride.

2. *Increase the length of each stride.* You will learn how to increase the strength and power of the muscles involved in sprinting to lengthen your stride without

reducing the number of steps you take per second.

3. *Improve your acceleration and start.* The training programs described in this book will improve both of these areas for your sport.

4. *Improve your sprinting form.* Although no two athletes sprint the same way, basic mechanics are similar for everyone. You will learn how to eliminate errors in arm action, body lean, foot contact, over striding, under striding, and tension to correct form problems that may be preventing you from sprinting faster.

5. *Improve your speed endurance.* Since you must complete many all-out sprints in your sport during competition, it is important to develop a high anaerobic conditioning level that allows you to do this without slowing down at the end of a long sprint or slowing down as the game progresses due to fatigue. With proper training, you will be able to complete each sprint at the same high speed throughout the game or match.

This is not a complicated plan. The training programs in your workout will increase speed in short distances by improving your performance in each of the five areas.

HOW TO USE THIS BOOK

Follow the steps listed below to get the most benefit from your 30-workout program:

1. *Identify your strengths and weaknesses.* In Chapter 1, you will be asked to complete several tests with the help of another person such as a parent, friend, or coach. Make a copy of the Test Score Sheet in Appendix A and analyze your scores. Record and compare the scores to the minimum "standard" presented to identify your weakness areas.

2. Read and practice the warm-up, stretching and cool-down routines presented in Chapter 2. You will complete these exercises before and after each of the 30 workouts.

3. Determine your current stage of growth and development with the help of a parent or coach. Your task is to make certain you have reached a physiological age that allows you to safely benefit from either the modified program for Early Adolescent athletes or the complete program for Late Adolescent and adult athletes.

Pre Adolescent Athletes - Athletes who have not reached the age of puberty and show no signs of developmental changes can safely engage in some training programs such as flexibility training (stretching), form training, modified speed endurance training and limited sprint-assisted training to increase stride rate. Programs such as plyometric training, weight training, speed-strength training, and sprint loading are not recommended.

Early Adolescent Athletes - The beginning of adolescence involves the growth spurt at the onset of puberty. Rapid growth of the long bones (arms and legs) takes place and changes body proportions. In females, puberty begins with breast development, presence of pubic hair, followed by first mensuration; in males by the level of development of secondary sex traits such as facial hair, pubic hair and genitals. There is also an increase in muscle mass in boys and body fat in girls. These changes usually take place between 10 1/2 - 12 years of age in females and 12 1/2 - 14 years of age in males

It is never too early to teach young athletes how to sprint.

although some individuals will not reach this stage until 2-3 years later. Since boys and girls are more likely to be injured during this period, training programs must be carefully supervised. Some programs, such as weight training, also produce very little increase in muscle strength and size in pre and early adolescent athletes due to low levels of testosterone and are not helpful at this early age. Prior to the Late Adolescent period, young athletes should devote most of their time to skill development in their sport, learning proper starting and sprinting form, and practicing various forms of sprint-assisted training suitable for their age level. The modified speed improvement program for early adolescent males and females in this book are designed to prevent unnecessary injury, avoid interference with growth and development and lay the foundation for the complete speed improvement program that begins in Late Adolescence.

Late Adolescent and Adult Athletes - The slowing or end of the growth spurt and the presence of secondary sex traits for several years suggests that the athlete is in the late adolescent or adult stage of growth and development and ready to respond to more vigorous training.

Keep in mind that age is a poor indicator of maturity at any stage of growth and development prior to the adult years and should only be used as a guide. Wrist X-ray and other tests may be done by a physician to more accurately determine the end of the growth spurt in both males and females. This normally occurs after age 13-14 in females and 15-16 in males although some individuals may not reach this stage until 2-3 years later. Athletes at this stage of growth and development should follow the complete speed improvement program presented in Chapter 8.

4. Read and study Chapters 3-7 until you understand how each training program works and what the program is trying to accomplish. You will have the opportunity to practice each exercise, drill, and

program in early workouts.

5. Follow the 30 Workouts in Chapter 8 as carefully as possible. You may need to return to the earlier chapters at times if there are drills or exercises you do not understand.

Remember! Every athlete can get faster. Young athletes in the past have improved their 40-yard dash time by more than 8/10 of a second. You can do the same. This book covers all aspects of speed improvement for athletes in most sports in a short, practical manner. Information is based on the author's 30 + years of research and "hands on" speed improvement training at all levels of competition. Complicated descriptions and diagrams have been eliminated in favor of a "JUST DO-IT" approach that allows you to immediately begin to develop a faster "YOU" that can pave the way to success in your sport.

1

A SERIES OF TESTS TO GET YOU STARTED:

HOW TO FIND YOUR STRENGTHS AND WEAKNESSES

Ask a parent, friend or coach to help you complete the simple tests described in this chapter. Your test results serve two important purposes: to locate weakness areas that are keeping you from sprinting faster, and to measure your progress throughout the 30-workout program.

Before you complete the first speed test, it would be helpful to master the information in the boxed area (Training Tips: 40-Yard Dash Clinic) in Chapter 6 to make certain you are taking full advantage of proper starting and acceleration techniques that can affect your score. You may want to ask a coach, parent or friend to help you master these techniques.

TEST YOURSELF

As you complete the tests described below, keep in mind that you are not competing against anyone. Your only purpose is to find out what factors are keeping you from sprinting faster. Get rid of all inhibitions and give every test your best effort. The more accurate your test scores, the more likely you are to be successful in the 30-workout program. Stop reading and take a moment to make a copy of the Test Score Sheet in Appendix A and place it on a clipboard or in a notebook to make it easier to record your scores.

Stationary 120-yard dash

Set-up and Equipment Needs. Stretch a finish cord with a handkerchief or flag draped over it at the measured distances of 40, 80, and 120 yards on a field or track. Place one timer with a stopwatch at each of the three finish tapes.

Test Procedure. Use a 3-pt. football or 4-point track stance on a grass or track area and sprint 120 yards through all three finish tapes. Timer #1 stands at the 40-yard mark and starts his watch on your first muscular movement and stops it when the flag on the tape at the 40-yard mark moves (as you touch that finish tape). Timer #2 stands at the 80-yard mark, starts his watch when the flag at the 40-yard mark moves and stops it when the flag at the 80-yard mark moves. Timer #3 starts his watch when the flag at the 80-yard mark moves and stops it when the flag at the finish line moves. Record your 40-yard time (by Timer #1), Flying 40 (time elapse from the 40 to the 80-yard mark by Timer #2), Speed Endurance (time elapse from the 80 to the 120-yard mark by Timer #3), and your Stationary 120-yard time (combined times of all three timers) on your Test Score Sheet.

What Your Scores Mean. With only one 120-yard sprint, you

already know a lot about yourself. Since every athlete can improve their *40-yard dash* score, regardless of their time in this test, YES is already checked (√) in the weakness column on your Test Score Sheet. We will use your remaining 120-yard sprint scores later.

Stride Length

Set-up and Equipment Needs. Place two markers (cones, posts, or sticks) 25 yards apart on a smooth dirt surface such as a baseball infield. Place a third cone 40 yards from the first cone to mark the starting line. Ask two helpers to stand within the 25-yard cones on the dirt surface with one tape measure.

Test procedure. Begin your run from a standing position at the starting cone, 40 yards from the other two cones. Make certain you are sprinting at full speed when you reach the second cone. On your first trial, two helpers will find your foot prints and measure the length of your stride from the tip of the left toe to the tip of the right toe as you sprint through the 25-yard area. On the second trial, the measurement is taken from the tip of the right toe to the tip of the left toe. This provides two unique aspects of stride length and allows a comparison of the push-off power from the left foot on one trial and from the right foot on the other trial to identify a possible muscle imbalance. Repeat the above procedure (trials 1 and 2) and record the average of the two runs for each push-off foot to the nearest inch on your Test *Score Sheet.* Avoid over striding or making exaggerated jumps from one foot to the other and sprint past the last cone using your normal form.

What Your Score Means. Take a moment to compare the length of your stride to other athletes of similar height to see if you fall within the ideal range by using the information below.

Ideal Range:

Males: 1.14 X height in inches + or - 4 inches

Females: 1.15 X height or 2.16 X leg length

Example: Bill is 5'4" tall (64") and has a stride rate of 58"

Bill's ideal stride length range is 1.14 X 64 or 72.96 (73 inches) + or - 4" or **69 - 77 inches** (73 minus 4 = 69, 73 + 4 = 77)

If you are within the range for your height and observers are not noticing under or over striding, you are likely to be close to your ideal stride length for your current form and strength and power in the muscles involved in sprinting. If your stride length is less than the lower range, check YES (√) in the weakness column on your Test Score Sheet. You are under striding and need to engage in specific training to lengthen your stride. Keep in mind that almost everyone can increase their stride length 3-6" without reducing the number of steps taken per second.

Now compare the length of your stride with a left foot push-off to the length with a right foot push-off. If there is a difference of more than 2-3 inches, a muscle imbalance exists that needs to be corrected. The imbalance can be confirmed by comparing the scores of your right and left leg on the kick-back strength-power test described later in this chapter. Strength training exercises similar to the push-off (kick-back, toe rises, plyometrics) can be used to correct the imbalance.

Stride Rate
(Steps taken per Second)

You can now use your Flying 40-yard and Stride Length test scores to find out how many steps you take per second by following the example below:

Example: John, age 14 has a stride length of 64" and completed the Flying 40-yard dash in 5.0 seconds.

Step #1: Divide 1440 (inches in 40 yards) by the length of your stride.

1440 divided by 64 = 22.5 steps to cover 40 yards

Step #2: Divide the number of steps taken in 40-yards by your Flying 40 Time.

22.5 divided by 5.0 = **4.5** (number of steps John takes per second)

Record your Stride Rate on the Test Score Sheet.
What Your Score Means. Since almost everyone can benefit

from improved stride rate, YES is checked (√) in the weakness column on your Test Score Sheet. This will be a key area of emphasis on your speed improvement program.

Acceleration

Test Procedure. Find your acceleration score by subtracting your Flying 40-yard time from your Stationary 40-yard time and record the results on the Test Score Sheet.

What Your Score Means. The difference between the 40-yard dash and the Flying 40-yard dash is your "Acceleration" time. If there is more than 7/10 of a second difference between these scores, check YES (√) in the weakness column on the Test Score Sheet. Your acceleration is poor and needs to be improved.

Testing Tip: One way to find our how fast you should now be sprinting a 40-yard dash is to add 7/10 of a second to your Flying 40-yard time. For example, if your stationary 40-yard time is 4.9 and flying 40 is 4.0, you should be sprinting the stationary 40-yard dash in 4.7 (Flying 40 of 4.7 + 7/10 of a second = 4.7). The 2/10 second difference is probably due to faulty starting techniques.

Speed Endurance

Test Procedure. Subtract your time from the 80-120-yard mark from your Flying 40-yard time and record the result on the Test Score Sheet.

What Your Score Means. By comparing the 40-to 80 to the

80-120-yard dash time, you can evaluate your *Speed Endurance*. This score determines whether you can make repeated 40-yard sprints during actual competition in your sport without slowing down due to fatigue. It also shows whether you will slow down at the end of a long sprint. If your Flying 40-yard time and the time elapsed from the 80-120-yard mark (also a flying 40) differ by more than two-tenths of a second, check YES (√) in the weakness column of your Test Score Sheet.

Testing Tip: A more advanced speed endurance test involves completing six 40-yard dashes at 30-second intervals (NASE Repeated 40s test), listing the times, and looking for the drop-off. If a difference of more than 3/10 of a second exists among any of the six sprints, check YES (√) in the weakness column.

Explosive Power and Quickness

Standing Triple Jump

Test Procedure. From a standing broad jump position with your feet at shoulder width, jump forward off both feet as far as possible, landing on only one foot before immediately jumping to the opposite foot, taking one final jump, and landing on both feet. Practice the standing triple jump at low speeds until you master the technique. The movement is the same as the triple jump in track and field, except for the two-foot takeoff. Record the best of five trials on your test score sheet.

What Your Score Means. The standing triple jump provides

an estimate of fast-twitch muscle fiber percentage in key areas without resorting to a muscle biopsy. The test also provides an indication of your genetic potential to become a fast sprinter. A good score on this test is 20' (middle school males), 25' (high school males), and 28' (college males); and 15', 20, and 23' for middle school, high school, and college females. Keep and mind that scores can be improved with training and you are not doomed to a life of the "slows" if scores are low in young athletes. If your score falls below the standard for your age, check YES (√) in the weakness column of your Test Score Sheet.

Quick Feet Test

Test Procedures. Place 20 two-foot-long sticks on a grass or artificial turf field exactly 18" apart for a total distance of ten yards. Pump your arms vigorously and use little knee lift while sprinting the ten yards by placing one foot between each stick without touching the sticks. The timer starts the stopwatch when your foot touches the ground between the first and second stick and stops the watch when contact is made with the ground beyond the last stick. Record the best of two trials on your test sheet.

What Your Score Means. This test provides an indication of your potential to execute fast steps and quick movements. An acceptable score is 3.8 or less seconds (middle school males), 3.3 (high school males), and 2.8 (college males) and 4.2, 3.8, and 3.4 for middle school, high school, and college females. If your score falls below the standard for your age, check YES (√) in the weakness column of your Test Score Sheet.

Quick Feet Test

Leg Strength

Set-up and Equipment Needs. Locate a Universal Gym, Nautilus or similar equipment with a leg press station that places you in a seated position.

Test Procedure. Adjust the seat on the leg press station until both legs are at right angles. Find the amount of weight you can press for just one repetition. On the first attempt, try an amount of weight equal to two times your body weight. If that amount is too little or too much, rest 3-4 minutes and add or remove weight before trying again. Continue to add or remove weight until you locate the amount, to the nearest 5-10 pounds, that you can leg press only one time. Record that amount on the Test Score Sheet.

What Your Score Means. You should slowly progress until you are capable of leg pressing 2 1/2 times your body weight. If you weigh 150 pounds, for example, your leg press score should be at least 375 pounds (150 X 2.5 = 375). If your score is less then 2.5 times your body weight, check YES (√) in the weakness column of your Test Score Sheet. You need to increase your leg strength.

Testing Tip: The leg press and score standard in this chapter does not apply to preadolescent or early adolescent athletes. These young athletes should also avoid all 1RM strength testing described in this chapter for the leg press and hamstring/quadriceps muscle groups.

Hamstring/Quadriceps Strength

Set-up and Equipment Needs. Locate a Universal Gym, Nautilus or similar equipment that has a leg curl and leg extension station.

Test Procedures. Use the same procedure described for the leg press to find your 1RM and record the results on the Test Score Sheet. Test each leg separately for both the leg extension and leg curl tests.

What Your Score Means. Your leg curl (hamstrings) scores should be close to 80% of your leg extension (quadriceps) scores. If you are capable of performing one leg extension repetition with 50 lb., for example, you should be able to complete one leg curl with 40 lb. of weight (80% of 50 = 40). If your leg curl score is less then 80% of your leg extension score, check YES (√) in the weakness column. You need to increase the strength of the hamstring muscles. If the hamstrings or quadriceps muscles are weaker in one leg than the other, check YES (√) in the weakness column of your Test Score Sheet. You need to increase the strength of that leg.

Push-off Power

Set-up and Equipment Needs. Locate a Universal Gym, Nautilus or similar equipment that has a leg press station.

Test Procedures. The single-leg kickback test measures the force you exert against an area similar to a starting block and the ground during the accelerating phase of sprinting. It also allows you to compare the force exerted by each leg. Stand to the side of a leg press station, facing away from the leg pad. Place one foot on the pad and bend your knee to a right angle before exerting as much force as possible to reach a full leg extension. Repeat the procedure until you find your 1RM (amount of weight you can extend for one repetition), then switch legs.

What Your Score Means. If the right and left leg scores differ by more than five pounds, a muscle imbalance exists that is significantly reducing your stride length every-other stride and your overall speed in short sprints. Check YES (√) in the weakness column of your test score sheet in Appendix A. Emphasize this exercise, toe rises and plyometrics in your training until improvement is noted.

Testing Tip: The average leg curl score in 1,345 middle school and high school football players tested in our speed camps was only 56% of the leg extension score. Pay close attention to your scores. The strength of the hamstring muscle group is the weak link in sprinting and needs to be improved in almost every athlete. You must slowly increase the strength of your hamstring muscles during the 30-workout period.

IDENTIFYING YOUR WEAKNESS AREAS

Now that you have completed and recorded your test scores, make certain you have identified your weakness areas by checking YES (√) if a test result reveals a weakness and NO (√) if a weakness does not exist. Complete the remaining portion of the Test Score Sheet to identify the training programs needed to correct these weaknesses.

YOUR NEXT STEP

Congratulations on completing the testing program. You now know a lot about yourself and the factors that are keeping you from sprinting faster in your sport. It is time to do something about it. Move on to Chapter 2 and master the proper warm-up, stretching, and cool-down methods you will use before and after each workout.

2

WARM-UP, STRETCHING AND COOL-DOWN:
HOW TO PROTECT AND PREPARE YOUR BODY FOR EACH WORKOUT

To avoid injury and make sure you complete the testing and training sessions at the highest performance level possible, it is important to warm-up correctly, complete a series of dynamic stretching exercises before each workout, and cool-down and stretch properly at the end of the workout.

WARM-UP

The warm-up period should contain two important parts: large muscle activity to raise body temperature 1-2 degrees and a stretching routine using dynamic exercises. These two aspects will prepare you for any vigorous workout.

Large Muscle Activity

There are many acceptable ways to prepare for a speed

training workout. You should begin with an easy paced, enjoyable jog for one-half mile or two laps (800 meters) completing the run in 7-10 minutes. Pick up the pace in the third lap and complete the run at 1/2 to 3/4 speed for the final 100 meters. Other variations of warm-up are included in your 30-workout schedule.

Once you are perspiring freely, you are ready for the dynamic stretching exercises.

Flexibility Training (Stretching)

Your stretching session will:

√ prepare you for the vigorous sprinting in your workout,

√ increase your range of motion in various joints,

√ aid muscle relaxation and help you sprint more efficiently and reach the maximum length of your natural stride with the least amount of resistance,

√ help prevent under striding due to inflexibility by improving the range of motion in the ankles, hips and shoulders, and

√ help prevent muscle strains and soreness and loss of motion when recovering from an injury.

Stretching and Flexibility Training Tips:

• Flexibility training (stretching) is a separate workout that must be taken seriously, not a token warm-up or warm-down.

• It is important to avoid stretching cold muscles and risking the chance of injury. Always complete a general warm-up session and make certain you are perspiring freely before stretching.

• Dynamic stretching exercises are completed in the beginning of each workout following the general warm-up session to prepare athletes for more vigorous sprinting activities. Static stretching exercises are completed at the end of each workout to increase range of motion.

• Static stretching exercises should involve both sides of the body with a goal of achieving near equal range of motion on both sides. Research suggests that a joint that is 15% more flexible than the corresponding joint is two and one-half times more likely to be injured.

• Static stretching exercises that may damage the joints should be replaced with a safe alternative exercise for that body part. If you still use any of the stretches on the Hit List described in this chapter, eliminate those exercises immediately.

When to Stretch. The proper procedure prior to a sprint training workout or workout in any sport is to complete a general warm-up routine to raise body temperature and follow with 8-12 minutes of dynamic stretching exercises such as jogging in place, butt kickers, sprint-arm movements, low-to-high knee lifts, and other specific movements of sprinting or movements in the sport or activity to follow. To improve flexibility in various joints, a second stretching session involving static exercises is used at the very end of each workout as part of the cool-down activity.

What Stretching Technique to Use. Just prior to your workout, concentrate your efforts on *dynamic stretching* only. This technique involves the ability to use the range of joint movement needed during physical activity (sprinting) while progressing from low to normal to high speed. Stretching movements are nearly identical to a specific activity such as sprinting, jumping, throwing, serving, or movements in a sport. Exercises are performed with the limbs moving to near full range of motion and slowly progressing to the high speed used in the sport or activity. Forget the traditional stretching exercises you have done in the past that involve holding a stretch for 30-60 seconds. Researchers have discovered that using static stretching exercises in the beginning of a workout reduces the force output potential of stretched muscles by 8-15% for as long as one hour. This reduction in muscle strength may also increase the likelihood of an injury. Your task is to complete a series of dynamic stretching movement such as those described later in the chapter prior to each workout.

The *static stretching* method is safe and effective <u>when used at the end of a workout, following the cool-down period.</u>

For each exercise, concentrate on two unique phases of static stretching: *easy stretching* for one repetition, in which you move slowly into the stretch and apply mild tension with a steady, light pressure, and *developmental stretching* for one to two repetitions in which you increase the intensity for an inch or less, easing off the stretch if the tension does not diminish. Breathe normally and avoid holding your breath.

How Much Intensity to Use. Exercises should involve a slow, relaxed, controlled, and pain-free movement for both dynamic and static stretching. Forget the "no pain, no gain" mentality. Dynamic stretching involves a progression from slow to moderate to high speed work for each movement. Static stretching should be done at a low intensity level of 30-40% of your maximum exertion. When using the static stretching technique at the end of a workout, you will learn to judge each exercise by the "stretch and feel method," easing off the push if pain is too intense. This type of stretching also helps injured tissue recover and breaks down scar tissue between muscles and tendons.

How Long to Perform each Stretch. Dynamic exercises such as jogging in place involves 2-3 sets of 10-15 slow repetitions with a low knee lift, resting 30 seconds before moving to a moderately faster speed and higher knee lift for 2-3 sets. A final set or two is completed with a waist high knee lift at 3/4 speed or more. A similar progression is used for other dynamic sprint specific leg and arm exercises. To improve flexibility using the static stretching method, you must remain in the hold position at the end of the stretch for a minimum of 30 seconds for the stretch to progress from the middle of the muscle belly to the tendons. Shorter "holds" will not increase range of motion. The "ideal" length of the hold is closer to 60 seconds. Your program begins with a 30-second hold and adds 3-4 seconds each workout until you can comfortably maintain the position at your maximum range of motion for 60 seconds after 3 weeks. In early workouts, it is important to count the seconds until you learn to stretch by the way it feels without having to count. Depending on the number of exercises, a static stretching session during the cool-down period will take about 10-12 minutes.

How Often to Stretch. The first stretching session using dynamic exercises takes place in the beginning of each workout immediately after the general warm-up to prepare you for high speed training and the second session, using static stretching exercises, is part of the cool-down activity at the end of the workout. This static stretching session focuses on improving range of motion.

How Flexible to Become. A gymnast, ballet dancer, and hurdler must be more flexible than a sprinter or athlete in team sports. The added flexibility of a yoga trainer will not improve speed and may actually increases the chances of injury. The flexibility exercises in your program are designed for sprinters and will safely increase the range of motion for high speed work.

What Exercises to Use. The following dynamic stretching routine involves the use of specific sprinter's exercises (Olympic form drills) after a general warm-up period in the beginning of your workout to prepare you for high speed work (see Chapter 6 for a photo and explanation of each exercise).

1. Jog-stride-sprint in place. Begin with a slow jog

in place using only a slight knee lift; complete three sets of 15-30 steps. Rest for 30-45 seconds before increasing the pace and raising the knees to waist level each repetition for three sets of 15-20 repetitions.

2. Single leg Cycling

3. Butt Kickers.

4. Wall Slide

5. Down-and-Offs

6. Pull-throughs. Complete three sets of ten repetitions with each leg at half speed.

7. Stick Drill

8. African Dance

9. Drum Major

10. Ankling

11. Sprint-arm Exercise - In a standing position with arms and hands in the relaxed sprinting position, move the arms through one complete cycle (right hand and arm forward to shoulder level, left hand back to the hip and repeat to complete one repetition). Complete two sets of ten repetitions at medium speed.

12. Complete 1-2 sets of exercises #1-11 at near maximum speed.

13. Complete a series of trunk and shoulder rotation movements at medium speed.

A good static stretching program should involve as many of the major joints as possible: neck, shoulders, back, hips, knees, wrists, and ankles. It is also important that exercises are as specific to the activity of sprinting or a particular sport as possible. The following routine involves a well-rounded selection of static stretches to complete at the end of your workout for athletes involved in speed training:

1. *Neck* - Bend forward at the waist with both hands on your knees and gently roll your head.

2. *Hamstring group (back of upper leg):* #1—Stand erect with both knees bent slightly. Bend over and touch the ground, holding the maximum stretch position. #2—Lie on your back, sit up and reach for the toes with both knees slightly bent, holding your maximum stretch position. Keep the knees slightly bent in both exercises to remove the pressure from the lower back. #3—Modified hurdler's position—Sit on the floor with the lead leg (right) extended and slightly bent at the knee. Bend the left leg 90 degrees toward the inside of the right leg until the sole of the left foot is touching the right knee. Pull yourself forward slowly and hold that position by grasping the right ankle. Reverse the legs and repeat.

3. *Quadriceps group (front of upper leg):* #1 Stand on the right leg, grasp the left ankle with the right hand. Instead of pulling, try to straighten the left leg. #2 Perform a single knee lunge by placing one leg in front of the body and extending the other behind. Bend forward at the trunk as you bend the lead leg to right angles. Reverse the legs and repeat both stretching exercises.

4. *Hip:* Lie on your back, relax and straighten both legs. Pull the left foot toward the chest and hold. Repeat using the right foot.

5. *Groin:* Assume a sitting position with the soles of the feet together. Place your hands around the ankles and pull, allowing both knees to move outward away from the body.

6. *Calf:* Stand about 1-2 feet from a wall and lean forward with the lead leg bent and the rear leg extended, placing the forearms on the wall and supporting the head in your hands. Move the hips forward keeping the heel of the straight leg on the ground until you feel a stretch in the calf. Reverse the lead and repeat the stretch.

7. *Achilles tendon and soleus:* Stand approximately two feet from a wall or fence. Bend both the rear and front knee slightly. Keep both heels on the ground and lean forward to get a much lower stretch. Reverse the lead leg and repeat the stretch.

Exercises to Avoid. When a joint is bent beyond your ability to control it with muscle strength, there is a risk of tearing muscles, tendons, or ligaments that support the joint or damaging the joint surface. The so-called "hit list" below includes outdated, potentially dangerous exercises that have been used in the past and have been replaced by equally effective, safe stretching moves described in the previous section. These stretching exercises should be avoided.

1. *Yoga Plow*—Athletes lie on their back, arms to the side, and bring both legs straight overhead until touching the ground. Football players are often asked to dig the tips of the shoes into the ground with a running motion. This is one of the most dangerous exercises ever used that puts stress and strain on the blood vessels to the brain, the upper spinal cord, and spinal disks and ligaments.

2. *Hurdler's Stretch*—Athletes sit on the ground with one leg extended in front and the other at right angles to the side in the hurdler's position and attempt to bend forward and lay the chest on the thigh of the lead leg. This exercise overstretches the muscles and ligaments in the groin and can cause chronic groin pull, injure the knees (meniscus cartilage and the medial collateral ligament) and irritate the sciatic nerve.

3. *Knee stretch*—Athletes rest on their knees with the lower legs underneath, then lean back until their head is on the ground. This stretch exceeds the skeletal range of motion of the knees and overstretches the patellar and collateral knee ligaments, destabilizing the knee.

4. Duck walk and deep knee bend—Walking like a duck in a deep knee bend position is very likely to damage the knees.

5. *Straight-leg toe touching*—This movement overstretches the posterior longitudinal ligament, a

main supporter ligament of the spine. Disks can also be damaged. The back muscles give little support during the straight-leg toe-touch movement and the sciatic nerve is in danger of being pulled from its connection.

6. *Ballet stretches*—Placing an extended leg in front of the body resting on a bar and bouncing forward is hazardous to the sciatic nerve, low back ligaments, muscles, joints and disks.

7. *Straight-leg raises*—Raising a fully extended leg overhead while lying on your back stretches the sciatic nerve beyond its normal limits.

8. *Straight-leg sit-ups*—This exercise is similar to the standing toe-touch except that you begin in a sitting position. After siting up 30 degrees, you are doing a hip exercise, not an abdominal exercise. Beyond that point, abdominal muscle strength is not improved. Bent-leg sit-ups and variations of the crunch are more effective and safer.

9. *Fast neck circles*—Increases the risk of pinching discs and overstretching delicate ligaments.

10. *Straddle jumps*—Jumping jacks that cause the feet to land further apart than shoulder-width can strain the knees.

COOL-DOWN

The cool-down phase is used at the end of a workout after completing repeated all-out sprints or other speed endurance training programs. It is important to allow the body to slowly return to normal by using 5-10 minutes at the end of each work-out to complete a slow jog for 1-2 laps around a track at a pace of 5-10 minutes per lap, with each lap slower than the previous one. This approach will also help prevent muscle cramps and mini-mize muscle soreness the following day. Static stretching exer-cises can now be used to increase your range of motion.

YOUR NEXT STEP

Read Chapter 3 and learn about the programs that will improve your stride rate.

3

IMPROVING STRIDE RATE:
HOW TO TAKE FASTER STEPS

The two main training programs designed to improve stride rate are Sprint-assisted Training and Strength-Power Training. Regardless of your test scores, stride rate training must be an important part of your workout. This phase is also the most fun. You will experience the feeling of raw power and be amazed with the results. With sprint-assisted training, you run a 40-yard dash faster than Olympic sprinters, Maurice Green and Tim Montgomery, NFL Speedster Michael Vick, MLB's Kenny Lofton, or John Harper of the Outer Banks of North Carolina.

World class sprinters have a stride rate of about 4.5 (females) to 5 (males) steps per second. Women sprint the 100-meter dash about 6/10 to 8/10 of a second slower than males mainly due to slower stride rates and differences in strength and power. Children take faster steps than adults. As height and leg length increases, stride rate decreases. There is no real advantage to having short or long legs. Long legs do allow a longer stride, but slower stride rate. Short legs result in a faster stride rate and shorter strides. It also takes a lot more strength, power, and energy to move long legs through the complete cycle in sprinting than it does shorter legs. Studies show that the ability to take fast steps is not so common in young athletes. Among 13-14 year old students, only fifteen had high stride rates. Approximately ten youngsters in 100 had a very short down time of 0.90 to 0.105 seconds (the support phase when one foot is contacting the ground). The important thing to remember is that stride rate can be increased regardless of your height or the length of your legs.

Pay close attention to your leg press, leg curl and leg extension test scores. Strength training improves stride rate by changing the ratio of strength to body weight in the muscles involved in sprinting. It also eliminates any strength imbalances found between the hamstring and quadriceps muscles and in the strength of other muscles in the left and right leg, ankle and foot.

Read this chapter carefully until you understand how sprint-assisted and the speed-strength training programs work. You will then be able to follow these programs in your 30-workout schedule.

SPRINT-ASSISTED TRAINING

Sprint-assisted training increases stride rate by forcing you to take faster steps than you can take without assistance. These exercises expose both the nervous and muscular systems to higher muscle contraction rates. Research shows that the number of steps an athlete takes per second and the length of the stride will improve after four to six weeks of sprint-assisted training.

You can choose from four basic methods. Some require special equipment and others do not. Since not all are equally effective, be certain to include towing as the main approach. The exact routines for each method are included in the 30-workout schedule in Chapter 8

Towing with Surgical Tubing

Towing

Towing or pulling athletes to sprint faster is not a new approach. Before the use of surgical tubing and two-person pulley arrangements, motor scooters, motor cycles and even automobiles were used.

Surgical Tubing. You can purchase a 20 foot piece of surgical tubing with two belts for as little as $39.95 (NASE,

Box 1784, Kill Devil Hills, NC 27948). The opposite end of the tubing can be fastened to another athlete, a tree or goal post so you can train alone. You only have to back up and stretch the tubing 20-30 yards before sprinting with the pull.

Surgical tubing is used at the owner's risk and adequate supervision is recommended at all times by a coach or parent. Although tubing rarely breaks, belts can work loose when improperly tied and cause injury. Tears can also occur if the tubing is stretched too far (more than 6 times the original length). These safety guidelines should be followed at all times:

1. Make certain the tubing is tied securely to the belt. After tubing is used a few times, the knots will tighten. Newly tied belts must be tightened and inspected before each run.

2. After putting on the belt, there will be an extra length of leftover belt (the "tail"). It is important to wrap the tail around the stomach, then thread it again through the loop formed before pulling securely to form a KNOT. This process should be repeated until most of the leftover belt is used. In other words, attach the belt properly, then tie several additional knots with the tail.

3. Inspect the tubing on the first run by letting it slide through your hand as you back up to locate a nick or rough mark. If a nick is detected, discard and replace with a new tubing.

4. Avoid stretching the tubing more than six times its length.

5. Avoid standing with the tubing fully stretched for more

than 1-2 seconds. It is during this stretched phase that knots come lose.

6. Avoid assuming a 3-point stance with tubing fully stretched. If the opposite end comes lose, it could recoil to the face and eyes.

7. Warm-up properly before using surgical tubing to avoid soft tissue injury. Jog at least one half mile, stretch thoroughly, and use a sequence of 20-25-yard walk-jog-stride-sprint segments for one fourth to one half mile. Avoid an all-out sprint the first several workouts if you are not in serious training.

Towing and other sprint-assisted training programs occur early in the workout immediately after your general warm-up and stretching exercises and before you are fatigued from drills, scrimmage, calisthenics, or other conditioning routines. Almost full recovery should occur between each repetition.

At a the end of each tow, it is important to attempt to sprint another ten meters at the high speeds attained without the pull. Some devices will allow you to uncouple after receiving the full benefits of the pull.

Some of the specific workout drills in the 30-workout program include the following:

1. Attach tubing to a goal post. Within 3-5 trials, back up an extra five yards each trial to increase the pull as you adjust to running at one-half speed the first three trials and increasing to no more than three-quarter speed for the remaining two.

2. Allow the tubing to pull you at approximately 4/10 of a second faster than your best 40-yard dash time. It takes only a slight pull to produce this effect. Place two marks 40-yards apart and have a partner use a stop watch to get your time for a 40-yard tow.

3. Two-Person Drill up and down the field. Tubing is attached to two runners. One runner (belt is turned around so tubing is attached to the belt at his back) sprints about 30 yards ahead against resistance and stops; the runner who provided resistance (tubing attached to the belt in the front) now sprints toward the stopped runner in his overspeed run. Continue for 75-100 yards before reversing roles.

4. Repeat the previous drill with runners sprinting backwards.

5. One athlete in tow races another who is not assisted by tubing. Reverse the situation and compare the difference. Race one of the fastest athletes against one of the slowest (neither being towed). Now tow the slower runner in a race against the faster runner who is not being towed.

6. Repeat drill #1 and emphasize high knee lift while under tow.

7. Repeat drill #1 and emphasize short strides and quick feet. Measure one of your strides before placing 20 sticks at a distance 6" shorter than your stride. Repeat drill #1 emphasizing rapid stride frequency.

The Ultra Speed Pacer. This method uses a thin elastic cord and pulley system. Two athletes lock on their belts with one sprinting at a 45 degree angle away from the pulley and the other toward the pulley to receive considerable assistance. The outgoing sprinter controls the degree of pull at a 2 to 1 ratio. The device has the potential to produce very high stride rates and speed.

Downhill Sprinting

If you can locate a 50-meter area with a slope of no more than 3 to 7 degrees (only a slight decline), you can vary your program with downhill sprinting. Keep in mind that too much slope will increase the risk of falling, cause over striding, landing on the heels of the feet, and ground contact beyond the center of gravity that produces a "braking effect" and causes you to sprint slower. The ideal area should allow a 20-meter sprint on a perfectly flat surface to accelerate to near-maximum speed, followed by a 15-meter high speed sprint downhill on a slope of 3-7 degrees (to force higher than normal stride rates and speed), and end with a 15-meter flat area (to allow you to "hold" the higher speed without the assistance of gravity). Ask your coach or parent to help find the right area.

High Speed Stationary Cycling

Since wind resistance, gravity, and body weight are eliminated, high speed stationary cycling allows an athlete to complete more revolutions (similar to steps in sprinting) per second than the sprinting action. This is a good sprint-assisted technique that should be used with one other method, such as towing or downhill sprinting.

Sprint-assisted Training Tips:

• A solid conditioning base of speed endurance training and weight training is necessary before beginning a sprint-assisted program.

• The concept of "work fast to be fast " is applied to sprint-assisted training and all other training programs.

• To sprint as fast as possible and be fatigue-free, the rest period between each repetition listed in your 30-workout schedule should be carefully followed.

• It is important to maintain proper form on all repetitions and avoid breaking form and sprinting out of control.

• After sprinting with the assistance of a pull or decline, it is important to try to maintain that high speed for another ten meters without assistance.

• Because of the longer stride, high knee lift and heel kick, and faster stride rates, muscle soreness is common after early workouts. Soreness should disappear in the second and third week.

• Towing should only be used on a soft, grassy area after the surface has been inspected for broken glass and other objects.

• Although untested, combining sprint-assisted with sprint-resisted training and finishing the workout with regular maximum effort sprints is a form of "contrast training" that targets an athlete's neuro motor patterns and help improve speed.

STRENGTH TRAINING

The drive of the supporting leg during the sprinting action takes about 0.09 to 0.11 second. Unfortunately, maximum strength in contracted muscles takes much longer (0.7 to 0.9 second) and you do not use anywhere near 100% of your strength during the sprinting action, except in the start and "drive" or acceleration phase. Weight training that improves speed-strength (ability to develop force rapidly) therefore, has the best chance of decreasing the supporting leg ground contact time and improving maximum mph speed. The 30-workout schedule includes a speed-strength training program that is designed to train the muscles to apply force rapidly and accelerate the body to maximum speed as fast as possible.

The leg extensors and flexors, ankle flexors and hip extensors and flexors are the muscles targeted in your speed-strength weight training program. The exercises will specifically train the fast-twitch muscle fibers and convert more of the intermediate fast twitch fiber to the fast twitch fiber responsible for improving sprinting speed. With proper training, almost all of your type 11a fibers can be converted to the faster type 11b fiber in these muscle groups. Keep in mind also that speed is dependent on the number of fast twitch fibers. Off-season training that places too much emphasis on distance running (endurance) will convert some of your fast type 1-b fibers to the slower II-a fibers. Although aerobic fitness is an important foundation, the workout schedule in this book avoids this problem for the 30-workout period during the in-season and off-season maintenance period by limiting distance training and emphasizing high speed sprint training programs.

Before beginning the speed-strength training program, you must develop a solid strength foundation. If you are an adolescent or adult-age athlete and have been involved in a weight training program for two months or more with 3-4 workouts weekly consisting of both upper and lower body exercises, you may either skip Micro Cycle #1 (Foundation Program) in Chapter 8 and begin with Micro Cycle #2-Speed-Strength or complete the three week program before moving on. Younger early adolescent athletes will remain with the Foundation Strength training program for the entire 30 workouts. Strength training is not recommended for preadolescent males and females.

Speed-Strength Training

Your speed-strength program has several objectives:
√ to develop the required force and tissue capacity for your sport,
√ to improve your leg strength/body weight ratio,
√ to improve hamstring and quadriceps strength and remove imbalances between muscle groups in the left and right leg,
√ to improve the speed-strength of the muscles involved in the start, acceleration and sprinting phase, and
√ to train the fast twitch muscle fibers and convert intermediate fibers to fast twitch fibers.

Specific exercises, the amount of weight to be lifted, number of repetitions and sets, length of the rest interval, and speed of contraction shown in the 30 Workout Schedule include the use of Periodization to make sure maximum benefits occur at the right time for your sport. The program trains the fast twitch muscle fiber which requires a rather heavy load (weight) for each exercise and rapid, explosive movements through the range of motion. A light load will not activate fast twitch muscle fibers regardless of how fast muscles are contracted.

The Dorsi Flex. "Plantar flexion" exercises such as the leg press, toe rise, uphill and stair case sprinting are used by most athletes to strengthen the bulky, lower part of the calf and are very important for sprinters and athletes in all sports. Unfortunately, athletes fail to strength train the front part of the lower leg through the use of "dorsi-flexion exercises" which are also critical for the proper balance of strength in the lower leg, prevention of shin splints, and the improvement of sprinting speed and jumping.

Unlike plantar flexion exercises that involve pushing the toe or top of the foot away from the knee to strengthen the calf muscles (gastrocnemius and soleus), dorsi flexion movements involve resistance while pulling the top of the foot toward the knee to strengthen the muscles lying in front of the lower leg (tibilias anterior, extensor digitonia, and peronous longus).

You can add these key strength training exercises to your workout by using the Dorsi Flex; one of the few inexpensive devices available to strengthen the smaller, weaker muscles in the front of the lower leg. This apparatus allows a variety of strength training movements essential to athletes in all sports that require sprinting and jumping. With only one ten lb. weight, you can increase the resistance up to 30 lb for each exercise. If additional weight in needed, a 25 lb. weight can be moved to add as much resistance as 75 lb.

The Dorsi Flex is available through the National Association of Speed and Explosion.

Strength Training Tips for Young Athletes:

• Weight training programs are different for young early adolescent boys and girls who are not well into or through the growth spurt. The two approaches are clearly separated for early adolescent and late adolescent and adult athletes in this Chapter and Chapter 8 and it is important to follow the guidelines. While the use of rather heavy weight (1-5RM) for each exercise, near maximum muscular contractions, 3-7 sets, and low repetitions in some micro cycles is desirable for older athletes, the approach is unsafe for younger athletes who should train with lighter weights, higher repetitions, and near full recovery between sets.

• The Power Lifting Federation suggests young people begin weight training at around age 14 for males, slightly younger for females. Since every child is different, age is not a solid guide for determining physical and mental readiness. If you need help in making this determination, consult a physical education instructor, a professional trainer, or a physician.

• Explosive force is the basis for strength training for sprinting and sports. Exercises should be completed at high speed throughout the range of motion.

• The best exercises are specific to movements in sprinting and involve the same muscle groups in the same manner.
• Training with free weights requires a workout partner or spotter at all times.

Exercises for Early Adolescent Athletes

Periodized strength training in the ten-week 30-workout macro cycle for athletes in the early adolescent period of growth and development and those who have not previously been involved in weight training emphasizes a well-rounded program and use of the general exercises listed below for the legs, back, shoulders, chest, arms, trunk, and abdomen, starting at 60% of the RM (repetitions maximum). Special weight machines are recommended since they are somewhat safer than free weights when proper supervision is provided.

Foundation Program:

Leg and Back Exercises: leg press, leg extension, leg curl, seated row,
Shoulder and Arm: Bench press, arm curls, lat pull down, bent-arm fly, shoulder press, and triceps extension.
Sprinter's exercises: Same as those described for Late adolescent and adult athletes.
Trunk/Abdomen: See exercises for the lower and upper abdominal muscles in Appendix C

Exercises for Late Adolescent and Adult Athletes

For late adolescent and adult-age athletes who already have developed a solid strength foundation from regular participation in weight training, the Micro cycle I foundation program is continued for only three weeks before being replaced with Speed-strength training and the addition of the Olympic Lifts in Micro-cycle 2. The program should be based on free-weight movements rather than isolated movements of special weight machines. Although some machine exercises are valuable, functional strength and speed-strength are better developed with free weights, exercises can more closely mimic sprinting movements, and a greater variety of sprint-type exercises are possible.

Foundation Program Exercises
(see Figure 3.1)

Group I: Bench press, power cleans, bent arm flys, dumbbell rowing, military press, two-arm curl, standing or seated triceps, front squat, lunge, heel raise.

Alternate Group: Incline bench press, dead lift, barbell rowing, shoulder shrug, bent-over lateral raise, reverse curl, wrist curl, one dumbbell heel raise.

The Olympic Lifts: Clean (barbell/dumbbell), Jerk (barbell, dumbbell, and machine rack), and Snatch (barbell) and dumbbell:

Sprint-arm Exercise

Knee Block Exercise

Sprinter's Exercises:

1. *Sprint-arm exercise (with dumbbells):* rapid sprinter's movement of the arms in 4-count cycles are performed with 5-10 lb weights.

2. *Kickback on a leg press station:* from a sprinter's starting position with the leg bent at right angles, a forceful thrust is exerted backward against resistance.

3. *Knee lifts against resistance on leg machine:* with the leg nearly extended in the standing position, a powerful upward thrust of the knee is made against resistance to bring the knee as high as the waist.

4. *Pull or "paw" downs on a leg machine:* In a standing position, one leg is placed over the top of the pad and a powerful pull down movement is exerted against resistance to bring the leg to an extended position.

5. *Trunk/Abdomen:* See the exercises in Appendix C.

a. Paw Down

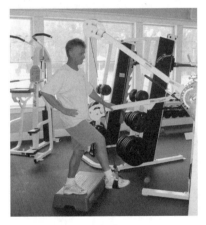

b. Paw Down

c. Paw Down

Figure 3.1 Strength Training Foundation Program Exercises

Bench press

Equipment: *Barbell, bench rack, spotter*

Movement: *Using an overhand grip, slowly lower the bar to the chest, then press back to the starting position.*

Hints: *Bend knees at 90^0 and keep feet off the bench and the floor.*
Muscle Groups: Pectoralis major, Anterior triceps, Deltoid

Incline bench press

Equipment: *Incline bench, squat rack, spotter*

Movement: *Using an overhand grip, slowly raise and lower the bar to the chest (both feet flat on the floor).*

Hints: *Use a weight rack to support the weight above the bench. Avoid lifting the buttock or arching the back while lifting.*

Muscle Groups: *Anterior pectoralis major, Anterior deltoid, Triceps.*

Power Cleans

Equipment: *Barbell*

Movement: *Using an overhand grip, pull the bar explosively to the highest point of your chest. Rotate hands under the bar and bend your knees. Straighten up to standing position. Bend the arms, legs, and hips to return the bar to the thighs, then slowly bend the knees and hips to lower to the floor.*

Hints: *Grasp the bar at shoulder width. Start with knees bent so hips are knee level. Keep head up and back straight.*

Muscle groups: *Trapezius, Erector spinae, Gluteus, Quadriceps*

Deadlift

Equipment: *Barbell*

Movement: *Using a mixed grip, bend knees so hips are close to knee level. Straighten knees and hips to standing position. Bend at knees and hips to return.*

Hints: *Keep the head up and back flat. Grasp bar at shoulder width.*

Muscle Groups: *Erector spinae, Gluteus, Quadriceps*

Bent arm flys

Equipment: *Dumbbells*

Movement: *Using an underhand grip, hold a dumbbell in each hand above the shoulders with the elbows slightly bent.*

Hints: *Keep elbows slightly bent at all times.*

Muscle groups: *Pectoralis major*

Barbell rowing

Equipment: *Barbell*

Movement: *Using an overhand grip, hold the barbell directly below your shoulders. With elbows leading, pull the barbell to chest and hold momentarily. Then slowly return to the starting position.*

Hints: *Grasp bar slightly wider than shoulder width. Refrain from swinging or jerking the weights upward to the chest region.*

Muscle Groups: *Latissimus dorsi, Rhomboid, Trapezius*

One dumbbell rowing

Equipment: *Barbell*

Movement: *Using an underhand grip, kneel with one hand and one knee on exercise mat. Pull weight on support side upward on chest.*

Hints: *hold dumbbell briefly at chest before returning.*

Muscle Groups: *Latissimus dorsi*

Shoulder shrug

Equipment: *Barbell*

Movement: *Using an overhand grip, elevate both shoulders until they touch the earlobes, then relax and return bar to the thighs.*

Hints: *Keep the extremities fully extended. Heavy weights (within limitations) will bring more rapid strength gains.*

Muscle groups: *Trapezius*

Military press

Equipment: *Barbell*

Movement: *Using an overhand grip, slowly push bar overhead from chest until both arms are fully extended.*

Hints: *Keep neck and back erect, and knees extended and locked.*
Avoid jerky movements and leaning.

Muscle Groups: *Deltoids, Triceps*

Upright rowing

Equipment: *Barbell*

Movement: *Using an overhand grip, raise the bar to the chin, and then return to thighs.*

Hints: *Grasp bar 6 to 8 inches apart. Keep elbows higher than the hands. Maintain an erect, stationary position.*

Muscle Groups: *Trapezius*

Bent-over lateral raise

Equipment: *Dumbbells*

Movement: *Using an overhand grip, grasp dumbbell in each hand and draw arms to shoulder level. Slowly return to hanging position.*

Hints: *Keep knees and elbows slightly bent. Hold weights for 1-2 seconds before returning to hanging position.*

Muscle Groups: *Posterior Deltoid, Latissimus Dorsi, Rhomboids*

Two-arm curl

Equipment: *Barbell*

Movement: *Using underhand grip, raise bar from thighs to chest level, and return.*

Hints: *Keep body erect and motionless throughout.*

Muscle Groups: *Elbow Flexors*

Reverse curl

Equipment: *Barbell*

Movement: *Using overhand grip, raise bar from thighs to chest lever, and return.*

Hints: *Use less weight than in two-arm curl.*

Muscle Groups: *Upper Arm Flexors, Hand Extensors, Finger Extensors*

Seated dumbbell curl

Equipment: *Dumbbells*

Movement: *Using an underhand grip, curl one or both dumbbells to the shoulder, then slowly return the weight to the sides of the body.*

Hints: *Keep the back straight throughout the entire movement.*

Muscle Groups: *Elbow Flexors*

Close grip bench press

Equipment: *Barbell, squat rack, spotter*

Movement: *Using an overhand grip, slowly lower the barbell to the chest and press back to the starting position.*

Hints: *Grasp center of bar (hands 2 to 4 inches apart). Bend knees at 90°; keep feet off the bench floor so as to avoid arching the back. Keep elbows in; extend arms fully.*

Muscle Groups: *Triceps, Anterior Deltoid, Pectoralis Major*

Standing or seated triceps

Equipment: *Dumbbell*

Movement: *With both hands grasped around the inner side of one dumbbell overhead, lower the weight behind your head, then return.*

Hints: *Keep the elbows close together throughout the maneuver.*

Muscle Groups: *Triceps, Deltoid*

Barbell wrist curl

Equipment: *Barbell*

Movement: *Using an underhand grip, let the bar hand down toward the floor and then curl toward you.*

Hints: *Grasp center of bar (hands 2 to 4 inches apart). Keep forearms in steady contact with the bench while moving the weight.*

Muscle Groups: *Wrist Flexors*

Reverse wrist curl

Equipment: *Barbell*

Movement: *Using a overhand grip, and moving wrists only, raise bar as high as possible, and return to the starting position.*

Hints: *Grasp barbell at shoulder width. Movement should only be at the wrist joint.*

Muscle Groups: *Forearm Extensors*

Front squat

Equipment: *Barbell, squat rack, chair or bench, 2 to 3 inch board, spotters*

Basic Movement: *Using an overhand grip, flex legs to a 90o angle. Return to standing position.*

Hints: *Keep the heels up, and point the chin outward slightly. A chair or bench can be placed below the body (touch buttocks slightly to surface).*

Muscle Groups: *Quadriceps, Gluteals*

Lunge with dumbbells

Equipment: *Dumbbells*

Movement: *Overhand grip; alternate stepping forward with each leg, bending the knee of the lead leg, and lowering your body until thigh of the front leg is level to the floor. Barely touch the knee of rear leg before returning to the starting position.*

Hints: *Keep your head up and upper body erect throughout the exercise. Avoid bending front knee more than 90o.*

Muscle Groups: *Quadriceps, Gluteals*

Heel raise

Equipment: *Barbell, squat rack, spotters, 2 to 3 inch boards*

Movement: *Using an overhand grip, the body is raised upward to maximum height of the toes.*

Hints: *Alter the position of the toes from straight ahead to pointed in and out .Keep the body erect.*

Muscle Groups: *Gastrocnemius, Soleus*

One Dumbbell heel raise

Equipment: *Dumbbell, 2 to 3 inch board*

Movement: *Using an overhand grip, shift the entire body weight on the leg next to the dumbbell, and raise the foot off the floor behind. Raise the heel of the support foot upward as high as possible and hold momentarily.*

Hints: *A wall is useful for balance, but avoid using free hand for assistance.*

Muscle Groups: *Gastrocnemius, Soleus*

BASIC WEIGHT TRAINING TECHNIQUES FOR LATE ADOLESCENT AND ADULT ATHLETES

Lifting Form. The emphasis is on quality and perfect technique for each exercise and repetition, rather than quantity (number of repetitions). Proper form is stressed at all times.

Amount of Resistance (Weight). Your speed-strength training weight for each exercise will progress from 30-85% of the maximum amount of weight (RM) you can lift one time. This range allows for explosive movements throughout the range of motion.

Intensity or Speed of Completing Each Repetition. Your task is to "intend" to and "attempt" to exert maximum force through the entire range of motion for each repetition. Contractions should be explosive and maximal.

Number of Repetitions and Sets to Complete. Three to seven sets of each exercise are recommended. Sets include variations of the following: 1-3 repetitions at 85% of maximum effort, 3-5 repetitions at 80-85%, 5-8 repetitions at 70-80%, and 8-15 repetitions at 60%.

Amount of Rest Between Sets. Two to six minutes of recovery is used between each set.

Amount of Rest Between Workouts. The best results occur when you allow at least 48 hours of rest (alternate-day-training) between each workout. For split-body routines emphasizing the upper body one day and the lower body the next, it is possible to train 6 consecutive days before taking a day of rest.

Progression. The speed-strength program in Chapter 8 slowly increases the amount of weight you lift and the number of sets and repetitions you complete. The Progressive Resistance Exercise Principle is applied in numerous ways to make certain speed-strength gains occur throughout the 30-workout program.

YOUR NEXT STEP

Move on to Chapter 4 to learn about the training programs, in addition to Sprint-assisted training and strength training that will improve the length of your stride.

4

IMPROVING YOUR STRIDE LENGTH:
HOW TO TAKE LONGER STEPS

Since everyone is capable of taking longer strides, your 30-workout schedule includes each of the training programs in this chapter

As you can see from the example below showing a stride length increase of only six inches, even small changes make a big difference:

Stride Length	Stride Rate	Feet per Second	Approximate 40-yd.Time
Current 6 Ft. X 4.0 sps *		24	5.0
New (+6") 6'6" X 4.0 sps*		26.4	4.6

By increasing stride length just 6" without altering the number of steps taken per second, flying 40-yd. times improve

*steps-per-second

by as much as 4/10 of a second.

The training programs in this chapter will add to the length of your stride by increasing the strength and power of the knee extensors and plantar flexors muscles of the feet involved in the push-off and leg drive action away from the ground and developing sprinting form that permits a long, low stride. The power for the "drive" or acceleration phase" of sprinting comes from a pushing action off the ball of the foot. Flexibility training, sprint-assisted training, weight training, plyometrics and sprint loading can increase the speed-strength and power in the muscles involved in this push-off and lengthen stride without decreasing stride rate.

SPRINT-ASSISTED TRAINING

Use the exact sprint-assisted program discussed in the previous chapter. Sprint-assisted training has been shown to lengthen the stride of sprinters.

STRENGTH TRAINING

Use the exact strength training program discussed in the previous chapter. Your strength training program focuses on the key muscle groups involved in the start, acceleration, and maximum speed phase of sprinting.

PLYOMETRIC TRAINING

Plyometrics increase the strength and power of the muscles

involved in sprinting through a series of jumping, hopping, and bounding movements for the lower body and swinging, quick action push-off, catching and throwing weighted objects (medicine balls, shot put, sandbags), arm swings, and pulley throws for the upper body. Training is designed to bridge the gap between strength and speed by using a "down" time (foot-ground contact) less than that used during the actual sprinting action. The main objective is to improve the ability to generate maximum force in the shortest time.

Plyometric exercises are grouped by level of intensity to allow progression from one micro cycle to another. Most exercises closely resemble specific sprinting movements and can force similar muscle groups to work at high rates of speed.

The main concept of plyometrics (loading and unloading) is easy to understand and you will immediately see that you already apply it in many sports. When you cock your wrist or ankle just before throwing a baseball, hitting a baseball, shooting a basketball, kicking a soccer ball or football, swinging a golf club or executing any tennis stroke, you are loading or rapidly stretching the muscles to activate the stretch reflex. When you explosively complete the action and throw the ball, you are unloading (the stretch reflex sends a powerful message to the muscles causing them to contract faster and with more power). The same thing occurs when you jump or sprint.

Plyometric Exercises

The exercises and drills in this section involve the basic

jumps that are important to sprinting and correspond to the direction of sprinting movement. Some of the drills include a "down time" (ground contact) similar to the start and acceleration phase of sprinting and others involve a very short down time less than what occurs during the sprinting action.

For each exercise, try to shorten your ground contact time by immediately going into the next repetition of the jump. Ask your coach or training partner to help you learn the proper form for each jump.

Low Intensity Jumps
(Beginning Program)

Squat Jump: From an upright position, hands behind the neck, drop downward to a one-half squat position before exploding upward as high as possible. Land and immediately explode upward again.

Split Squat Jump: Same as above except you land with one leg extended forward and the other behind the center of your body (lunge position).

Double-leg Ankle Bounce: With arms extended to the sides, jump upward and forward using the ankles. Execute the next jump upon landing.

Lateral Cone or Bench Jump: Stand to one side of a cone or bench, jump laterally to the other side, jumping back to the starting position immediately upon landing.

Medium Intensity Jumps

Pike Jump: Begin in an upright position with both

arms to the side, feet shoulder-width apart. Complete a vertical jump as you bring both fully extended legs in front of the body and reach out with both hands to touch the toes (pike position). Go into the next jump immediately upon landing.

Double-Leg Tuck Jump: From the starting position described above, complete a vertical jump and grasp the knees while in the air, releasing the grasp before landing and immediately going into the next jump.

Standing Jumps - Standing Triple Jump: From the standing broad jump position, use a two-foot take-off to jump forward as far as possible, landing on the right foot; then immediately jump forward and land on the left foot. Finish with one last jump off the left foot landing on both feet. This is identical to the triple jump in track except for the use of a two-foot take-off.

Standing Jumps - Standing Long Jump: Use the initial jump described above with maximum arm swing, exploding into the next repetition upon landing.

Standing Jumps - Single-Leg Hop: From a standing broad jump position with one leg slightly forward, rock to the front foot and jump as far and high as possible driving the lead knee up and out. Land in the starting position on the same foot and continue jumping until you complete the number of repetitions specified.

Double-leg Bound: From the standing broad jump position, thrust both arms forward as the knees and body straighten and the arms reach for the sky.

Double-and-Single-leg Zigzag Hop: Place ten cones

20 inches apart in a zigzag pattern. Jump with the legs together in a forward diagonal direction over the first cone keeping the shoulders facing straight ahead. Immediately upon landing, change direction to move diagonally over the second cone, continuing until you have jumped 10 cones. Repeat using one leg at a time.

Alternate Leg Bound: Stand upright with one foot slightly ahead of the other. Push-off with the back leg as you drive the lead knee up to the chest and try to attain as much height and distance as possible. Continue immediately by repeating this action with the other leg.

Running Bound: Run forward and jump as high as possible on each step, emphasizing height and high knee lift and a landing with the center of gravity under you.

High Intensity Jumps or Short-Response Hops and Bounds

Double-leg Vertical Power Jumps: From the standing vertical jump position, thrust both arms upward and jump as high as possible, immediately jumping again upon landing with as little ground contact as possible.

Single-leg Vertical Jump: Repeat the above action using a one leg take-off.

Side Jump and Sprint: Stand to one side of a bench or cone with feet together. Jump back and forth over the bench 4-10 times. On the last jump, sprint forward for 25 yards.

Double-leg Speed Hop: Assume an upright position with the back straight, shoulders forward, and head up. Jump as high as possible, bringing the feet under the buttocks in a cycling motion at the height of the jump. Jump again immediately upon contacting the ground.

Single-leg Speed Hop: Repeat the above exercise taking off one leg only.

Decline Hop: From a quarter-squat position at the top of a grassy hill with a 3-4 degree slope, hop down the hill for speed using the double-leg hop.

Single-Leg Stride Jump: Assume a position to the side and at one end of a bench with only the inside foot on top of the bench, arms at your sides. Drive both arms upward as the inside leg on the bench pushes off to jump as high as possible. Continue jumping until you reach the other end of the bench.

Box Jumps: Step off a box of the correct height and immediately jump upward and outward upon hitting the ground.

Your plyometric program concentrates on the lower body. If time permits, add the medicine ball sit-up toss, medicine ball overhead backward throws, and underhand forward throws. Your weight training program will include the sprint-arm exercise (dumbbell arm swings).

Plyometric Training Tips:
• Safety Precautions: Unsound, unsupervised plyometric programs can cause shin splints, knee, ankle, and lower back problems.
• Preadolescent and early adolescent boys and girls should

avoid plyometrics.

• Avoid plyometrics at any age unless you meet the following strength standards: Lower Body - Leg press 1 1/2 to 2 times your body weight, Bench press your body weight.

• Use footwear with good ankle and arch support and a non-slip sole (basketball or aerobic shoe).

• Complete the workout on soft, grass areas, padded artificial turf, or wrestling mats; never on asphalt or gymnasium floors.

• Complete the general warm-up and stretching program before each plyometric workout.

• Avoid depth jumping from boxes higher than .75 meters.

• Too many workouts per week and too many jumps per workout may result in injury. Do not add to the workouts or number of jumps recommended in the 30 workout schedule.

• You must "train fast to be fast." Leading researcher, Paavo Komi, emphasizes that it is not the length of the stretch, but the quickness of the stretch that is important. This means hitting and getting off the ground as quickly as possible.

• Concentrate on an all--out effort on each jump, hop, or bound. You will not automatically sprint at maximum speed, serve at 100+ miles per hour in tennis, kick a ball 60+ yards, or jump 25+ feet without being "psyched" prior to the movement. You must concentrate on completing this task with your maximum effort.

• The most helpful plyometric exercises are those that closely resemble specific sprinting movements of the upper and lower body and involve the same muscle groups.

FORM TRAINING

Sprinting technique also plays a major role in the length of your stride. These factors are discussed in Chapter 6.

YOUR NEXT STEP

Move on to Chapter 5 to learn about the training programs used to improve the "drive" phase (acceleration) of sprinting.

5

IMPROVING ACCELERATION:
HOW TO START AND REACH
MAXIMUM SPEED FASTER

If there is more than 7/10 of a second difference between your Flying 40-yard score and the Stationary 40-yard score, you need to improve your acceleration. In addition to the leg press and leg extension tests, the standing long jump and the standing triple jump are used to evaluate explosive power or speed strength. Speed strength plays a major role in how fast you accelerate for the first 20 meters.

In most sports, athletes accelerate to full speed from either a "dead stop" or a slow jog most of the game. It is no surprise that the average speed players reach during competition are well below their maximum. On only a few occasions will you accelerate for 60 meters; the approximate distance it takes a world class sprinter to reach maximum speed. A home run in baseball, a 100m or 200m sprint in track, and a long run in football, rugby, soccer, field hockey or lacrosse could approach or exceed 60 meters. What is generally referred to as speed is actually acceleration to maximum speed and it is this quality that demands the most attention in most sports.

Five training programs are used to improve acceleration; three have already been presented in previous chapters (sprint-assisted training, plyometrics, and speed-strength training). Form training is discussed in Chapter 6. One additional program discussed in this chapter, Sprint Loading, allows you to train the specific muscle groups involved during the acceleration or drive phase of sprinting.

SPRINT LOADING

Sprint loading is a program that trains the muscles involved in the start and acceleration phase of sprinting using the resistance of a sled, a slight incline, or stadium stairs. These exercises require more effort than normal sprinting on a flat surface. Too much resistance, such as a 15-20 lb. weight will reduce speed by about 8 percent due to a decrease in stride rate (the support phase or ground contact time rises about 22 percent). Use of no more than 8-10 lb. of weight or no more than the ideal inclines described in this chapter for uphill sprinting will eliminate much of the problem and still force the biceps femoris and rectus femoris muscles to work harder than in all-out sprinting on a flat surface. This is one example of how "more weight" is not better. It is more important to load the key muscles involved in sprinting lightly and avoid drastic reductions in stride rate, stride length, and speed.

Choose one or two methods described below, depending upon the equipment available, and follow the program in Chapter 8 (Table 8.6).

1. *Uphill Sprinting:* Locate a 10-30 yard incline of 3-7 degrees.

2. ***Weighted Sleds, Weighted Vests, and Parachutes:*** Numerous inexpensive sleds can be purchased or a spare tire with a rope and belt can be made for little cost. Metal and plastic models are available that allow quick and easy weight changes. Weighted vests can be found that are loaded in half-pound increments. Small parachutes provide enough resistance without interfering with proper form during acceleration sprints. Younger athletes tend to enjoy parachutes more than the other sprint loading methods.

3. **Two-person harness:** Two athletes of similar weight use the same harness. One provides the resistance and the other the power.

4. **Surgical Tubing:** Partners can alternate sprinting against resistance.

5. **Stadium Stairs:** Stadiums or other stairs can be used in the same manner as uphill sprinting. Staircase acceleration training can be dangerous and should be avoided by young athletes since all-out sprints can result in a fall that produces a serious injury.

Sprint Loading Training Tips:
• Speed is developed more effectively when heavy physical loads are avoided. Use a load that still allows you to maintain high speed sprinting and ground contact times close to those in sprinting without resistance.

Resistance with Parachute   *Resistance with Weighted Vest*

Two Person Harness

• Use correct sprinting form on each repetition. If you are "breaking" form there is too much resistance.

• At the end of each repetition, try to uncouple the resistance and sprint for another 10-15 yards.

• Do not alter the distances and repetitions presented in your 30 Workout Schedule. The program has been tested and found effective in improving acceleration time.

• Sprint loading with lightweight vests can also be combined with sprint-assisted training such as towing or downhill sprinting.

• The best sprint loading equipment provides a quick release mechanism to allow an all-out sprint after 3-10 seconds of resistance.

YOUR NEXT STEP

Move on to Chapter 6 to learn about the training programs that improve sprinting form.

6

IMPROVING SPRINTING TECHNIQUE:
HOW TO DEVELOP PROPER FORM

Form training is another area that can help every athlete. Unless your "start" is perfect and sprinting form is "flawless," take the time to master the form drills described in this chapter and eliminate your major form errors.

Proper sprinting form is not a natural act. In fact, most athletes of all ages have some faulty traits that need to be corrected. No two athletes sprint exactly the same. There is also no perfect style that fits all body types. The key is to improve your basic technique without trying to mimic the exact form of others. You are an individual and must learn the ideals of form in theory and adapt them to your personal traits.

This chapter briefly covers key points to help improve your starting technique and acceleration and eliminate gross errors during the sprinting phase. Two to three 15-20 minute form training sessions per week with your coach or training partner should be enough to make a difference.

Read and practice the information in the Training Tips Box below to improve your 40-yd. dash scores by mastering the correct form in the start and acceleration phases of sprinting. If you are a football, soccer, or baseball player, your 40-yard or 60-yard time will heavily influence your coach. You will be surprised by how much you can improve by practicing these tips.

Training Tips: 40-yard dash Clinic

The timed 40-yd. and 60-yd. dash is used in football, basketball, soccer, baseball and other sports to evaluate players for different positions, to offer scholarships, and even to decide who makes the team and who gets cut. It has become the single most important test in team sports; yet the test is taken by athletes who know very little about proper starting techniques and the unique tips below that can immediately improve their time.

• Regardless of the starting technique you use, the stronger leg should be placed in the front position since the lead leg is responsible for about two-thirds of the velocity at the start. To identify your stronger leg, compare your scores in three tests: 1. single leg press, 2. single leg extension, and 3. single leg sprinter's kick-back (same as the weight training exercise described in Chapter 3; assume a sprinter's starting position with your back to the leg press station, place one leg bent at right angles on the push plate, exert explosive force backward for one repetition, adding weight until you find the maximum amount you can move one time only, repeat using the other leg).

• Master the medium track start and adapt it to the 3-point stance if you are a football player and feel more comfortable in that position. Place the front foot 14-21" behind the starting line with the knee of your rear leg almost even with the toe of the front foot. Get in a comfortable position with your weight back and arms, neck, and back relaxed. The arms should slant backward from the starting line with your head down, looking at the ground. When ready, shift your weight forward, then up. Lift the front knee 6-8" with the legs almost parallel to the ground. Your buttocks should be 3-5" higher than your shoulders. Shift forward to place tension on the hands for a short time only. Drive the left arm (bent at 90 degrees at the elbow) forward and up as you drive the right arm back only to your hip, then thrust it forward.

• A common error is to step forward with the back foot as the front foot pushes off. No track athlete would ever make this mistake. Near equal thrust off the front and back foot must be exerted to initiate the "drive" phase of sprinting and get out of the starting stance. The force exerted by the rear foot is about 75% of the force applied by the lead foot. This thrust off both feet occurs before the rear foot steps forward. To form the habit of pushing off both the lead and rear feet requires hours of concentrated practice. Have your workout partner block both feet with his feet and "tell" you about the thrust you are applying on each start.

• If possible, stay with the 4-point track start since it makes it easier to support your forward weight .

• Place a lot of weight on the hands. The best times occur when you almost "stumble" out of the start.

• Take 4-5 "falling form" starts in each of form training workouts with enough weight forward to cause you to stumble out of the blocks.

• Lean forward until your shoulders are over the line <u>while the right knee is still on the ground</u>. It is easier to hold your weight over the line in this position until you move to the "get set" position.

• Rise up slowly and maintain the "hold" or "set" position (keeping the shoulders over the starting line) only a very short time to reduce the strain on the hands and possibly surprise the timer who is reacting to your first muscular movement. Eyes should be fixed on the running surface as you maintain the "head down" position with as much forward lean as possible for the start and the entire "drive" or acceleration phase of your sprint.

• Wear spiked shoes to improve push-off power.

• If you are being tested on natural turf, dig two small holes in the ground to increase your traction during the push-off; or have a friend block both feet with their feet while standing behind you.

• The first movement is with the arms and involves an aggressive arm drive (one arm drives forward as the other moves backward).

• Use vigorous, smooth arm movement the first 10 yards; continue to work the arms hard throughout the sprint. To sprint fast, you must concentrate on sprinting fast; it does not occur automatically.

• Avoid straightening up too fast; stay low for the first 8 -12 yards with the head down.

• If you get a bad start, had a bad run or slipped, stop immediately and do not complete the run. Ask for another trial. If you complete the test, you may not get a second chance.

• Sprint 5-8 yards past the finish line rather than using the "lunge."

• In young, preadolescent athletes and early adolescent athletes, the standing start may be a better choice since it is often faster than the 3-pt. or 4-pt. start because of the lack of strength development necessary to drive out of the crouch position.

Medium Track Start

Each practice repetition of the start should cover a minimum of 10-15 meters or 8-10 strides. The brief check list below includes important aspects your coach or training partner can look for when analyzing your starting form and the acceleration phase of sprinting:

In the Preparatory Position

__Yes __No   Relaxed position with proper foot and
             arm spacing?
__Yes __No   Weight evenly distributed between hands, knees
             and feet?
__Yes __No   Straight arms are shoulder width apart?

In the "Set" position:

__Yes __No   Movement of the center of gravity above the
             front foot?
__Yes __No   Front leg bent at 90 degree angle?
__Yes __No   Hips slightly higher than the shoulders ?
__Yes __No   Both feet apply pressure to the ground/blocks?
__Yes __No   Straight arms shoulder-width apart and in front of
             the hands?

Take-off/starting action:

__Yes __No   Explosive thrust exerted off both the lead and
             rear foot?
__Yes __No   Rear foot leaves the ground/block first?
__Yes __No   Fast, flat forward swing of the rear leg?

The "Drive" or acceleration phase:

__Yes _No   Gradual straightening of the body and lengthening
             of stride?

__Yes __No   Landing on the balls of feet and limited lowering
of heels?

__Yes __No   Head down position looking at the ground?

SOUND MECHANICS OF SPRINTING

It is difficult to describe an ideal sprinting form for all athletes. Explanations are often too technical, difficult to follow, and unhelpful. The form drills and trouble shooting form tips in this chapter, combined with assistance from a track coach or training partner, will help eliminate most technique errors that are keeping you from sprinting faster.

Training Tip for Young Athletes:
Some experts believe that the preschool and early elementary school years are the most favorable for learning correct sprinting form. After age 7 or 8 children may have lost a unique opportunity to learn to sprint correctly. Although you can "teach an old dog new tricks," it is much more difficult to eliminate faulty form after bad habits have been used for so many years. The preadolescent and early adolescent period is an ideal time to develop proper form and correct form errors that will hinder your speed in the future.

Olympic Form Drills

With the help of your coach, training partner, or sprinter from the track team, take the time to master each of the form drills in this section. These drills will help establish a basic sprinting form that eliminates the wasted energy that does not contribute to forward movement. Although this will be difficult

a. Cycling   b. Cycling

and require weeks of practice, you will be able to take the important step of including the drills in each training session as a regular part of your warm-up.

Workout Drills. Complete two to three sets of each drill every workout.

Cycling. Leaning against a wall, bar or other support, one leg is cycled through in a sprinting manner. Emphasize keeping

Butt Kickers

the leg from extending behind the body, allowing the foot to kick the butt during recovery and pawing the ground to complete the action. Ten cycles with each leg make up one set.

Butt Kickers. Without moving the upper body very much, concentrate on heel hitting the buttocks as you jog forward. Ten kicks with each leg make up one set.

Wall Slide. From a jog, the action is the same as the butt kickers except the heel of the recovery leg must not travel behind the body. Imagine a wall of glass running down the back, and do not allow the heel to break the glass. This action will produce knee lift without forcing the action. Ten kicks with each leg make up one set.

Down-and-Offs. From a high knee position, the emphasis is to decrease foot/ground contact by hitting the ground with the ball of the foot and getting off rapidly. The effort on the ground should bounce the leg up into a high knee position. Ten down-and-offs make up one set.

Down and Offs

Pull-Throughs. Extending the leg in front of the body like a hurdler, the leg is brought down and through ground contact in a power motion. Ten pull-throughs with each leg make up one set.

Stick Drill. Twenty sticks (18-24 inches in length) are placed 18" apart on a grass surface. Athletes sprint through the sticks as fast as possible, touching one foot down between each. Emphasize high knee lift and quick ground contact. One run equals one set.

African Dance. While running forward, raise each leg to the side of the body as in hurdling, and tap each heel with your hand. A 10-yard run equals one set.

Drum Major. While running forward, rotate the leg inward to the midline of the body and tap the heel at the midline. A 10-yard run equals one set.

Drum Major

Ankling. Jog with short strides and emphasize the plantar flexion phase of ground contact and recovery as you strive to take faster steps with shorter ground contact time.

Starts and Acceleration. Complete 4-5 "falling form" starts with enough weight forward to cause you to stumble out of the starting position for your sport. Complete 4-5 starts from a slow jog and the crouch position for 10-15 meters or 8-10 strides.

Many additional drills can be used.

Pump and Stride Training

The pump and stride method will help improve stride rate and acceleration. Athletes complete three repetitions of 25-50 yards by bringing the knees toward the chest and gradually moving forward while vigorously pumping the arms. Twenty high knee pumps are completed every 10 yards. The emphasis is on rapid knee/arm pumping and high knee lifts. A series of 15-40 yard sprints from a slow jog, "crouch" and head-down position with rapid knee and arm pumps are used to improve acceleration. Team sport athletes jog slowly, quickly assume a crouch position, plant the outside foot and sprint vigorously in the opposite direction.

Form Tips: Troubleshooting Sprinting Mechanics

Arm Action. If your arms are tense, practice loose, swinging movements from a standing position. Remember to swing from the shoulder and keep the arms relaxed at all times. Although the arms work in opposition to the legs, they must be coordinated with the action of the legs for maximum sprinting efficiency.

Body Lean. Many athletes and some sport professionals suggest too much body lean. At maximum speed, the body should have a slight lean in the direction of the run. It is important to note that the lean comes from the ground and not from the waist. The lean is only a result of displacing the center of gravity in the direction of the run. Leaning by bending at the waist interferes with the correct mechanics of sprinting.

Foot Contact. Avoid running up on the toes. The toes have no power or stability and do not allow athletes to run fast. Start on the balls of your feet and push against the ground. Don't reach for and pull toward the ground; this strategy will develop injuries and result in poor sprinting mechanics and slow times. Allow the heel to make contact with the ground when running at any distance.

Over striding. Over striding is the worst and most misunderstood element of sprinting. Don't reach and over stride to increase stride length. Push against the ground and allow the foot to land underneath the center of gravity. Placement of the foot in front of the center of gravity will cause the body to slow down.

Under striding. Try not to be too quick. To much turnover will cause athletes to run fast in one place without covering much ground. Quality sprint speed is a combination of both stride frequency and stride length. One does not replace the other.

Tension. Don't try to power through a race or sprint effort. Athletes can not run fast when they are tight. To run fast it is important to stay relaxed.

Improvement. Your speed will improve as you establish and repeat well developed and efficient patterns of correct form each workout.

Source: *Sportspeed: The #1 Athlete Training Program, 3rd Ed.* (2003); Human Kinetics by George B. Dintiman, and Robert D. Ward, Human Kinetics Publishers.

YOUR NEXT STEP

Move on to Chapter 7 to learn about the training programs that will improve your speed endurance and keep you sprinting at maximum speed for the entire game or match.

7

IMPROVING SPEED ENDURANCE:
HOW TO GET INTO CONDITION TO
SPRINT SHORT DISTANCES

If your test scores show you are have a low level of speed endurance (more than 2/10 second difference between your flying 40-yard test score and your 80-120-yard score, or more than 3/10 second difference among six repeated 40-yard dashes completed at 30-second intervals), you need to include the two programs described in this chapter.

Speed endurance training will keep you sprinting at maximum speed over and over for the entire game or match without slowing down at the end of a long sprint or after sprinting many different times. It also provides you with the necessary foundation to complete the other training programs in the 30-workout schedule. You have seen football players tackled from behind by slower players, sprinters passed in the final 10-20 meters of a race, baseball players who run out of steam and are tagged out at home, or basketball players beaten to the ball by slower opponents. These things will not happen to athletes who develop a high level of speed endurance.

The speed endurance training program in the 30-Workout Schedule will be designed for your sport. How far you sprint, how many times you sprint and the amount of rest between sprints in each workout is designed to prepare you to sprint these distances over and over in your sport. You can easily improve speed endurance in 3-4 weeks by following your sports-specific program in the 30-Workout Schedule.

SPEED ENDURANCE
TRAINING PROGRAM

Interval Sprint Training. This method will be the main approach to improving speed endurance for repeated sprints in your sport. It is merely an organized version of "wind sprints," or "alternates," that you may have used in the past. The main difference is that careful records are kept to make certain you are progressively doing more work each training session. This is done by changing the length of each sprint, amount of rest between each sprint, number of sprint repetitions, length of the workout (time), and number of workouts per week; and making sure the program is similar to what actually happens during competition in your sport. Football players, for example, will complete 3-12 short sprints of 10-75 yards with 25-30 second rest intervals (length of the huddle). Athletes in other sports will use different distances and rest intervals.

Pick-up Sprints. This easy, effective approach is adaptable to all sports. An athlete jogs 25 yards, 3/4 strides 25 yards, sprints 25 yards and ends that set with a 25 yard walk. The walking phase provides the only rest period between sets. As improvement occurs, the distance is increased to segments of 40 and 60 yards. Sprinting longer distances is used along with a series of maximum effort drills (300 and 400m sprints, sprinting in place to exhaustion, and maximum effort jumps) at the very end of the workout.

Specific speed endurance workouts for various sports are presented in Chapter 8 (Table 8.4).

Speed Endurance Training Tips:

• Speed is hindered by fatigue. Your speed endurance program will delay fatigue during competition.

• The objective is to cover about the same or greater distances than those normally sprinted in your sport (football, rugby, soccer, lacrosse, field hockey, 20-60 yards, basketball, 10-30 yards, baseball, 30-120 yards, and tennis (5-15 yards). In addition, over-distance and maximum effort training are added to develop a high level of speed endurance.

• Repetitions of "maximum effort sprinting" for 30-60 seconds should be a part of everyone's speed endurance program.

• At least one maximum effort exercise to complete exhaustion should be included at the end of each speed endurance workout.

YOUR NEXT STEP

You are ready to start your 30-workout schedule. Move on to Chapter 8 to learn about the order in which each training program fits into your schedule and begin your first workout.

8

PUTTING IT ALL TOGETHER:
THE 30-WORKOUT PROGRAM

You now have a fair understanding of what to do to improve your speed. You have been tested, your scores have been evaluated, and you know what training programs are needed to make you faster. You are about to begin your program.

USING YOUR TRAINING PROGRAMS IN THE CORRECT ORDER

Although there are some differences of opinion among conditioning coaches, there is a logical and research-supported sequence for the placement of different training programs used in the same workout rather than as concentrated micro cycles.

The chart below presents the recommended order of use for the various training programs in each workout. After a *formal warm-up* routine, *dynamic stretching* exercises are combined with *form training*, followed by *sprint-assisted training* that must be done when your body is still fatigue free and capable of very high speed. All conditioning activities such as *calisthenics, speed endurance training, weight training, and plyometrics* are the last items on the workout schedule. A final 5-10 minute cool-down period is followed by static stretching exercises to end the workout.

Research also supports a system introduced by Italian coach, Carlo Vittori, for the proper order of use for the conditioning activities listed above: weight training, followed by plyometrics, and ending with a series of short all-out sprints. Your workout schedule uses a variation of this method in some sessions. Keep in mind that other approaches have also been shown to yield good results.

YOUR 30-WORKOUT SCHEDULE

Your workout schedule includes all the training programs necessary to improve stride rate, stride length, acceleration, form and speed endurance. The 30th workout gives you a chance to practice the "Maintenance Program" that is designed to keep you from losing your new found speed and gains in strength, power, form, speed endurance and stride rate and length. Each training program is presented in the 30-workout schedule in the suggested order described above. A fourth workout can be added if necessary to focus on a specific weakness area in a concentrated manner such as "speed day" that devotes a total workout to fast movements of the upper and lower body with 3-4 different forms of sprint-assisted training and speed-strength training.

The Complete Speed Improvement Program for Late Adolescent and Adult Athletes - Warm-up, Dynamic Stretching,

Recommended Order for Each Training Program
in Your 25-Workout Schedule

Training Program	Length (Min.)	Order	Fre-quency	Explanation
General Warm-up	8-12	1	Before each workout	Warm-up continues until you are perspiring freely. You are now ready to begin the stretching or flexibility session.
Dynamic Stretching	15-20	2	Once each	Complete one set of the Olympic Form & form drills at a slow-to-moderate pace (1/2 speed) followed by a second set at up to 3/4 speed to complete your dynamic stretching routine using sprint-specific movements. Emphasize starting/acceleration form and perfect sprinting form at all times as you complete each exercise that serves both as a dynamic stretch and form practice.
Sprint-assisted Training	10-25	3	2-3 weekly	Completed before you are fatigued from other conditioning programs. Rest between each repetition should result in near full recovery. The object is not to condition but to exert sub maximal stride rates and stride lengths.

Training Program	Length (Min.)	Order	Frequency	Explanation
Speed Endurance Training	15-20	4	2-3 weekly	The main objective is to improve your ability to make repeated short or long sprints in your sport without slowing due to fatigue.
Speed-strength Training	30-60	5	3 weekly	Conditioning items #6, #7, and #8 are grouped in sequence at the end of the workout. Although other systems are in use, research indicates that this order has both a practical and scientific basis.
Plyometrics	15-20	6	1-2 weekly	Plyometric exercises closely mimic the starting, acceleration and sprinting action and attempt to use a ground contact time shorter than that during the sprinting action.
Short all-out sprints	10-12	7	Each workout	A series of 4-10, 30-40 meter sprints are used.
Cool down and Stretching	15 - 20	8	Each workout	Light jogging and a static stretching session follows weight training, plyometrics and short sprints.

Form Training, Sprint-assisted Training, Speed Endurance Training, Sprint Loading, Speed-strength Training, Plyometrics, Short-all out sprints, Cool-down, and Static Stretching.

The Speed Improvement Program for Early Adolescent Athletes -Warm-up, Dynamic Stretching, Form Training, Modified Weight training (Functional strength foundation consisting of light weight and high repetitions), Sprint Loading (uphill sprinting only), Speed Endurance training (50% of the workout described), Sprint-assisted Training (30-50% of the workout described), Cool-down and Static Stretching.

The Speed Improvement Program for Preadolescents age 8-11 - Although a program for this age is not covered in this book, it is the ideal age to develop correct sprinting form through the use of a good Form Training Program that involves a coach or knowledgeable adult. The start and the "drive" phase is also important for young athletes to learn how to accelerate from a slow jog in a "crouched" position. By the time most athletes reach the Late Adolescent stage, they have so many flaws in their technique that it is difficult to ever achieve correct sprinting form. The poor form of 80-90% of young athletes is considered by many to be a flaw in the physical education system. This is also the age where stride rate reaches its all-time high and, according to Soviet sports experts, is the ideal time to use a modified sprint-assisted program such as towing. After 3-4 four weeks of form training and short distance speed endurance training, a sprint-assisted program can be used once weekly for three weeks followed by 1-2 times weekly for three weeks that involves about 1/3 to 1/2 of the repetitions shown in Table 8.3

Instructions:

1. Age group athletes should consult their physician on the status of their current health and stage of growth and development before beginning this training regime.
2. Workouts may be too strenuous for some individuals. Take full advantage of Cycle 1: preconditioning and acclimation and extend this period into another 2-3 weeks if workouts are too difficult. It is important to progress safely and slowly, at your own pace, until you are ready for the more vigorous training in cycles 2, 3 and 4.
3. Begin this program no later than 10 weeks before the start of the competitive season in your sport.
4. Follow the suggested order for each training program in every workout.
5. Depending upon the availability of equipment and exercise rooms, select either a Monday-Wednesday-Friday or Tuesday-Thursday- Saturday workout schedule.

Micro Cycle 1: Preconditioning and Acclimation Cycle   (3 Weeks: 9 workouts)

Monday-Wednesday-Friday or Tuesday-Thursday-Saturday Schedule

Use this three week cycle to leisurely experience each program, determine your strength training starting weights, master the correct technique for each weight training exercise and Olympic form drill and prepare yourself for the all-out high speed training in Cycle 2. A typical workout in this cycle can be completed in 90 minutes.

ACTIVITY	TIME (MIN)	SPECIFIC ACTIVITY

WORKOUT #1

Warm-up	8-12	Jog 1/2 mile (2 laps) in 8-9 minutes. In crease the pace to 1/2 speed the final 100 meters of each lap. Continue for a third lap or until you are perspiring freely.
Dynamic Stretching & Form Training	20	Complete one set of each Olympic form drill concentrating only on the correct technique: Wall slide, Cycling, Butt kickers, Down and Offs, Pull Through, African Dance, Drum Major, and Starts and Acceleration drills. Include practice starts and concentrate on ex- erting force off both feet. Have your coach or training partner help you. Be patient. Some movements are difficult to learn and it my take several weeks to master the drills. Complete a second set at a faster pace to complete your dynamic stretching routine.
Weight Training	45	Early adolescent athletes: Complete workout #1 in Table 8.1.
	30	Adolescent and adult athletes: Complete workout #1 in Table 8.2. Concentrate on learning "perfect" form for each exercise.
Static Stretching	10-12	Concentrate on mastering the proper form for each stretch; neck, hamstrings, quadriceps, hip, groin, calf, and Achilles tendon and soleus described in Chapter 2. Do each exercise on both sides of the body holding the stretch for 30 seconds with no bouncing or jerking. Take your time, relax, and stop if there is pain.

ACTIVITY	TIME (MIN)	SPECIFIC ACTIVITY

WORKOUT #2

Warm-up	8-12	Same as workout #1.
Dynamic Stretching & Form Training	20	Same as workout $1.
Weight Training	30	Adolescent and adult athletes: Complete workout #2 in Table 8.2 Continue to concentrate on learning "perfect" form.
Static Stretching	8-10	Same as previous workout. Increase the "hold" time to 33 seconds.

WORKOUT #3

Warm-up	8-12	Same as previous workout.
Dynamic Stretching and Form Training	20	Same as previous workout.
Weight Training	30	Early adolescent athletes: Complete workout #3 in Table 8.1.
	30	Adolescent and adult athletes: Complete workout #3 in Table 8.2.
Static Stretching	10-12	Same as previous workout. Increase the "hold" time to 36 seconds.

WORKOUT # 4

Warm-up	15	Jog 3/4 mile (3 laps) in 12-13 minutes. Continue for a fourth lap or until you are perspiring freely.

ACTIVITY	TIME (MIN)	SPECIFIC ACTIVITY
Dynamic Stretching & Form Training	20	Complete two sets of the Olympic form drills moving forward 20 yards on each exercise at one-half speed. Complete a third set of each exercise at a faster pace to complete your dynamic stretching routine.
Weight Training	30	Early adolescent athletes: Complete workout #4 in Table 8.1.
	30	Adolescent and adult athletes: Complete workout #4 in Table 8.2.
Static Stretching	10-12	Same as previous workout. Increase the "hold" time to 40 seconds.

WORKOUT # 5

Warm-up	15	Same as workout #4 or you may subsitute moderate activity in your sport for 15-20 minutes such as basketball shooting; passing, catching, kicking a football; kicking a soccer ball, tennis rallies, fielding and throwing in baseball; and other leisurely activities in your sport.
Dynamic Stretching & Form Training	20	Same as previous workout.
Weight Training	30	Adolescent and adult athletes: Complete workout #5 in Table 8.2.
Static Stretching	10-12	Same as previous workout. Increase the "hold" time to 43 seconds.

ACTIVITY	TIME (MIN)	SPECIFIC ACTIVITY

WORKOUT # 6

ACTIVITY	TIME (MIN)	SPECIFIC ACTIVITY
Warm-up	15	Same as previous workout.
Dynamic Stretching & Form Training	20	Same as previous workout
Sprint Loading	10	Low Intensity program designed to add some resistance to the muscles involved in sprinting. Complete workout #6 in Table 8.6.
Weight Training	30	Early adolescent athletes: Complete workout #6 in Table 8.1.
	30	Adolescent and adult athletes: Complete workout #6 in Table 8.2. Ask a weight training expert to check your form in each exercise.
Static Stretching	10-12	Same as previous workout. Increase the "hold" time to 46 seconds

WORKOUT # 7

ACTIVITY	TIME (MIN)	SPECIFIC ACTIVITY
Warm-up	15	Jog one mile (4 laps) in 12-16 minutes. Increase the pace to 1/2 speed to 3/4 speed striding the final 50 yards of each lap.
Dynamic Stretching & Form Training	12-15	Complete two sets of the form drills moving forward 20 yards on each exercise at one-half speed. Complete a third set of each exercise at a faster pace to complete your dynamic stretching routine. Now that you have mastered the technique, the drills can be completed in less time.
Sprint Loading	10	Complete workout #7 in Table 8.6.

ACTIVITY	TIME (MIN)	SPECIFIC ACTIVITY
Speed Endurance Training	15	First speed endurance session. Complete workout #7 in Table 8.4
Cool Down	5	Jog 1/4 mile in 3-4 minutes.
Weight Training	45	Early adolescent athletes: Complete workout #7 on table 8.1.
	35	Adolescent and adult athletes: Complete workout #7 in Table 8.2.
Static Stretching	10-12	Same as previous workout. Increase the "hold" time to 50 seconds.

WORKOUT # 8

Warm-up	15	Same as previous workout.
Dynamic Stretching & Form Training	15	Same as previous workout.
Weight Training	35	Adolescent and adult athletes: Complete workout #8 in Table 8.2.
Static Stretching	10-12	Same as previous workout. Increase the "hold" time to 53 seconds.

WORKOUT # 9

Warm-up	15	Same as previous workout.
Dynamic Stretching & Form Training	12-15	Same as previous workout.
Sprint Loading	10	Complete workout #9 in Table 8.6.

ACTIVITY	TIME (MIN)	SPECIFIC ACTIVITY
Speed Endurance Training	15	Complete workout #9 in Table 8.4.
Cool-down	3-4	Jog 1/4 mile in 3-4 minutes.
Weight Training	30	Early adolescent athletes: Complete workout #9 in Table 8.1.
	35	Adolescent and adult athletes: Complete workout #9 in Table 8.2.
Static Stretching	10-12	Same as previous workout. Increase the "hold" time to 56 seconds.

Micro Cycle 2: Speed-Strength Cycle (3 Weeks: 9 workouts)
Monday-Wednesday-Friday or Tuesday-Thursday-Saturday Schedule

This three week cycle emphasizes speed strength and moves into low intensity plyometrics, sprint-assisted training, sprint loading, and speed endurance training as your workout schedule develops into a near complete speed improvement program. A typical workout in this cycle can be completed in approximately two hours.

WORKOUT #10

Warm-up	15	Same as previous workout
Dynamic Stretching & Form Training	12-15	Repeat the previous Dynamic Stretching and Form training workout.
Speed Endurance Training	15	Complete workout #10 in Table 8.4.
Cool-down	7	Jog 1/4 mile in 3 minutes. Walk 1/4 mile in 4 minutes.
Weight training	30	Early adolescent athletes: Complete workout #10 in Table 8.1

ACTIVITY	TIME (MIN)	SPECIFIC ACTIVITY
	5	Adolescent and adult athletes: Complete workout #10 in Table 8.2. The focus now changes to speed-strength training and involves explosive movements through the range of motion, heavier weight determined by a percent of the maximum amount of weight you can lift one repetition and multiple sets that begin with 3 and increase to 7 in the next micro cycle.
Static Stretching	10-12	Same as previous workout. Increase the "hold" time to 60 seconds.

WORKOUT # 11

Warm-up	15	Same as previous workout.
Dynamic Stretching & Form training	12-15	Repeat the previous Dynamic Stretching and Form Training
Sprint Loading	10	Complete workout #11 in Table 8.6.
Weight training	50	Adolescent and adult athletes: Complete workout #11 in Table 8.2.
Plyometrics	15	Adolescent and adult athletes only: Follow the low intensity program beginning with workout #11 in Table 8.5. Concentrate on using correct form for each exercise. Early adolescent athletes: Not reccommended.
Short all-out sprints	15	2 X 30-meters with high knee action, 2 X 30-meters sprints with near complete recovery after each repetition.
Cool-down	7	Jog 1/4 mile in 3 minutes. Walk 1/4 mile in 4 minutes.

ACTIVITY	TIME (MIN)	SPECIFIC ACTIVITY
Static Stretching	15	Same as previous workout.

WORKOUT # 12

Warm-up	15	Same as previous workout.
Dynamic Stretching & Form Training	12-15	Repeat the previous Dynamic Stretching and Form Training workout.
Speed Endurance Training	15	Complete workout #12 in Table 8.4.
Cool-down	7	Jog 1/4 mile in 3 minutes. Walk 1/4 mile in 4 minutes.
Weight training	30	Early adolescent athletes: Complete workout #12 in Table 8.1.
	50	Adolescent and adult athletes: Complete workout #12 in Table 8.2.
Plyometrics	15	Adolescent and adult athletes: Complete workout #12 in Table 8.5. Early adolescent athletes: Not recommended.
Static Stretching	10-12	Same as previous workout. Complete each exercise two times.

WORKOUT # 13

Warm-up	12	Jog 3/4 mile (3 laps) in 10-12 minutes, increasing your speed to a striding pace (3/4 speed) the final 50 meters of each lap.
Dynamic Stretching & Form Training	12-15	Complete two sets of the form drills moving forward 20 yards on each execise at one-half speed. Complete a third set

ACTIVITY	TIME (MIN)	SPECIFIC ACTIVITY
		of each exercise at a faster pace to complete your dynamic stretching routine.
Sprint Loading	10	Complete workout #13 in Table 8.6.
Speed Endurance Training	15	Complete workout #13 in Table 8.4.
Cool-down	7	Jog 1/4 mile in 3 minutes. Walk 1/4 mile in 4 minutes.
Weight training	30	Early adolescent athletes: Complete workout #13 in Table 8.1.
	50	Adolescent and adult athletes: Complete workout #13 in Table 8.2.
Static Stretching	10	Second stretching session. Same as previous workout.

WORKOUT # 14

Warm-up	12	Same as previous workout.
Dynamic Stretching & Form Training	12-15	Same as previous workout.
Weight training	50	Adolescent and adult athletes: Complete workout #14 in Table 8.2.
Plyometrics	15	Adolescent and adult athletes: Complete workout #14 in Table 8.5. Early adolescent athletes: Not recommended.
Short all-out sprints	15	4 X 30-meters with high knee action, 4 X 30-meters sprints
Cool-down	7	Jog 1/4 mile in 3 minutes. Walk 1/4 mile in 4 minutes.

ACTIVITY	TIME (MIN)	SPECIFIC ACTIVITY

Static Stretching | 10 | Second stretching session. Same as previous workout.

WORKOUT # 15

Warm-up	12-15	Same as previous workout.
Dynamic Stretching & Form Training .	12-15	Same as previous workout.
Sprint Loading	10	Complete workout #15 in Table 8.6.
Speed Endurance Training	15	Complete workout #15 in Table 8.4.
Cool-down	7	Jog 1/4 mile in 3 minutes. Walk 1/4 mile in 4 minutes.
Weight training	40	Early adolescent athletes: Complete workout #15 in Table 8.1.
	50	Adolescent and adult athletes: Complete workout #15 in Table 8.2.
Static Stretching	10-12	Same as previous workout.

WORKOUT # 16

Warm-up	12	Same as previous workout
Dynamic Stretching & Form Training .	12-15	Same as previous workout.

ACTIVITY	TIME (MIN)	SPECIFIC ACTIVITY
Mid-workout Retest	45	Return to Chapter 1 and complete the following tests once again: Stationary 120-yard dash, Stride length, Speed Endurance, Leg Strength, Hamstring/ Quadriceps Strength. Record your scores on the Test Score Sheet in Appendix A and compare the results.
FREE PLAY OR	60	Practice the skills in your sport leisurely, play in a pick-up game, engage in the activity you enjoy the most, or complete the remaining training programs listed below.
Sprint-assisted Training	10	Complete workout #16 in Table 8.3. Do not exceed 1/2 of your maximum speed as you adjust to running with proper form while being "towed" or running downhill.
Cool-down	7	Jog 1/4 mile in 3 minutes. Walk 1/4 mile in 4 minutes.
Weight Training	45 50	Early adolescent athletes: Complete workout #16 in Table 8.1. Adolescent and adult athletes: Complete workout #16 in Table 8.2. New abdominal exercises are added for both groups.
Static Stretching	10-12	Same as previous workout.

WORKOUT # 17

Warm-up	12	Same as previous workout.
Dynamic Stretching & Form Training .	12-15	Same as previous workout.

ACTIVITY	TIME (MIN)	SPECIFIC ACTIVITY
Sprint-assisted Training	15	Complete workout #17 in Table 8.3. Do not exceed 3/4 of your maximum speed. Continue to focus on proper sprinting form.
Sprint Loading	10	Complete workout #17 in Table 8.6.
Weight Training	50	Adolescent and adult athletes: Complete workout #17 in Table 8.2.
Plyometrics	15	Adolescent and adult athletes: Complete workout #17 in Table 8.5. Early adolecent athletes: Not recommended.
Short all-out sprints	15	5 X 30-meters with high knee action 5 X 30-meters sprints
Cool-down	7	Jog 1/4 mile in 3 minutes. Walk 1/4 mile in 4 minutes.
Static Stretching	10-12	Same as previous workout.

WORKOUT # 18

Warm-up	12	Same as previous workout.
Dynamic Stretching & Form Training .	12-15	Same as previous workout.
Sprint-assisted Training	15	Complete workout #18 in Table 8.3. Do not exceed 1/2 of your maximum speed as you adjust to running with proper form while being "towed" or running downhill.
Speed Endurance Training	15	Complete workout #18 in Table 8.4.
Cool-down	7	Jog 1/4 mile in 3 minutes. Walk 1/4 mile in 4 minutes.

ACTIVITY	TIME (MIN)	SPECIFIC ACTIVITY
Weight Training	40	Early adolescent athletes: Complete workout #18 in Table 8.1.
	50	Adolescent and adult athletes: Complete workout #18 in Table 8.2.
Static Stretching	10-12	Same as previous workout.

Micro Cycle 3: Speed-Specific Cycle (2 Weeks: 6 workouts)

Monday-Wednesday-Friday or Tuesday-Thursday-Saturday Schedule

This two week cycle emphasizes the exercises in all training areas that mimic the sprinting action and involves the same muscles utilized to accelerate and reach maximum sprinting speed. A typical workout in this cycle can be completed in approximately two and one-half hours.

WORKOUT # 19

Warm-up	15	Jog 3/4 mile (3 laps) in 12-13 minutes, increasing your speed to a striding pace (3/4 speed) to maximum speed the final 50 meters of the second and third lap. Run 1/4 mile or one lap around the track using the following cycle: walk 20 yards, jog 20 yards, 3/4 stride 20 yards, and sprint 20 yards.
Dynamic Stretching & Form Training	12-15	Complete one set of each Olympic form drill covering 20 yards each exercise at 3/4 leg and arm speed and a second set at near maximum speed.
Sprint-assisted Training	15	Complete workout #19 in Table 8.3. Focus on correct sprinting form at all times.

ACTIVITY	TIME (MIN)	SPECIFIC ACTIVITY
Speed Endurance Training	20	Complete workout #19 in Table 8.4.
Sprint Loading	10	Complete workout #19 in Table 8.6.
Cool-down	10	Jog 1/2 mile in 6-7 minutes. Walk 1/4 mile in 4 minutes.
Weight Training	60	Adolescent and adult athletes: Complete workout #19 in Table 8.2.
Static Stretching	10-12	Same as previous workout.

WORKOUT # 20

Warm-up	15	Same as previous workout.
Dynamic Stretching & Form Training	12-15	Same as previous workout.
Weight Training	45	Early adolescent athletes: Complete workout #20 in Table 8.1. Specific speed-strength exercises for sprinters are added to each workout.
	60	Adolescent and adult athletes: Complete workout #20 in Table 8.2.
Plyometrics	15	Adolescent and adult athletes: Begin Medium Intensity Plyometrics by completing workout #20 in Table 8.5. Early adolescent athletes: Not recommended.
Short all-out sprints	20	6 X 30-meters with high knee action 6 X 30-meters sprints
Cool-down	10	Jog 1/2 mile in 6-7 minutes. Walk 1/4 mile in 4 minutes.
Static Stretching	10	Same as previous workout.

ACTIVITY	TIME (MIN)	SPECIFIC ACTIVITY

WORKOUT # 21

Warm-up,	15	Same as previous workout.
Dynamic Stretching & Form Training .	12-15	Same as previous workout.
Sprint-assisted Training	20	Complete workout #21 in Table 8.3.
Speed Endurance Training	20	Complete workout #21 in Table 8.4.
Sprint Loading	10	Complete workout #21 in Table 8.6.
Cool-down	10	Jog 1/2 mile in 6-7 minutes. Walk 1/4 mile in 4 minutes.
Weight Training	60	Adolescent and adult athletes: Complete workout #21 in Table 8.2.
Static Stretching	10-12	Same as previous workout.

WORKOUT # 22

Warm-up	15	Same as previous workout.
Dynamic Stretching & Form Training .	12-15	Same as previous workout
Sprint-assisted Training	25	Complete workout #22 in Table 8.3.
Speed Endurance Training	20	Complete workout #22 in Table 8.4.
Cool-down	10	Jog 1/2 mile in 6-7 minutes. Walk 1/4 mile in 4 minutes.

ACTIVITY	TIME (MIN)	SPECIFIC ACTIVITY
Weight Training	45	Early adolescent athletes: Complete workout #22 in Table 8.1.
	60	Adolescent and adult athletes: Complete workout #22 in Table 8.2.
Plyometrics	15	Adolescent and adult athletes: Complete workout #22 in Table 8.5. Early adolescent athletes: Not recommended.
Static Stretching	10	Same as previous workout.

WORKOUT # 23

ACTIVITY	TIME (MIN)	SPECIFIC ACTIVITY
Warm-up	15	Same as previous workout.
Dynamic Stretching & Form Training .	12-15	Same as previous workout.
Sprint Loading	10	Complete workout #23 in Table 8.6.
Weight Training	45	Early adolescent athletes: Complete workout #23 in Table 8.1.
	60	Adolescent and adult athletes: Complete workout #23 in Table 8.2.
Plyometrics	15	Adolescent and adult athletes: Complete workout #23 in Table 8.5. Early adolescent athletes: Not recommended.
Short all-out sprints	20	Same as previous workout.
Cool-down	10	Jog 1/2 mile in 6-7 minutes. Walk 1/4 mile in 4 minutes.
Static Stretching	10-12	Same as previous workout.

ACTIVITY	TIME (MIN)	SPECIFIC ACTIVITY

WORKOUT # 24

Warm-up	15	Same as previous workout.
Dynamic Stretching & Form Training .	12-15	Same as previous workout.
Sprint-assisted Training	25	Complete workout #24 in Table 8.3.
Speed Endurance Training	20	Complete workout #24 in Table 8.4.
Cool-down	10	Jog 1/2 mile in 6-7 minutes. Walk 1/4 mile in 4 minutes.
Weight Training	60	Adolescent and adult athletes: Complete workout #24 in Table 8.2.
Static Stretching	10-12	Same as previous workout.

**Micro Cycle 4: High Intensity Speed-Specific Cycle
(2 Weeks: 6 workouts)**

**Monday-Wednesday-Friday or Tuesday-Thursday-
Saturday** Schedule

This two week cycle moves you into the high intensity phase of each training program and ends with one leisurely workout to allow you to become familiar with your maintenance program which is designed to prevent you from losing any of the gains acquired in the previous nine weeks as you enter the competitive season in your sport. The maintenance phase requires 1-2 workouts weekly. A typical workout in this cycle can be completed in less than three hours.

ACTIVITY	TIME (MIN)	SPECIFIC ACTIVITY

WORKOUT # 25

Warm-up	15	Same as previous workout.
Dynamic Stretching & Form Training	12-15	Same as previous workout. Ask your partner or coach to complete one final check on your technique in each drill and exercise.
Sprint-assisted Training	30	Complete workout #25 in Table 8.3.
Speed Endurance	20	Complete workout #25 in Table 8.4.
Cool-down	10	Jog 1/2 mile in 6-7 minutes. Walk 1/4 mile in 4 minutes.
Weight Training	45	Early adolescent athletes: Complete workout #25 in Table 8.1.
	60	Adolescent and adult athletes: Complete workout #25 in Table 8.2.
Static Stretching	10-12	Same as previous workout.

WORKOUT # 26

Warm-up	15	Same as previous workout.
Dynamic Stretching & Form Training .	12-15	Same as previous workout.
Sprint-assisted Training	30	Complete workout #26 in Table 8.3 using a stationary cycle to obtain high leg turnover.
Speed Endurance Training	20	Complete workout #26 in Table 8.4.

ACTIVITY	TIME (MIN)	SPECIFIC ACTIVITY
Cool-down	10	Jog 1/2 mile in 6-7 minutes. Walk 1/4 mile in 4 minutes.
Weight Training	60	Adolescent and adult athletes: Complete workout #26 in Table 8.2.
Plyometrics	20	Adolescent and adult athletes: Begin high intensity plyometrics by completing work out #26 in Table 8.5. Early adolescent athletes: Not recommended.
Static Stretching	10	Same as previous workout.

WORKOUT # 27

ACTIVITY	TIME (MIN)	SPECIFIC ACTIVITY
Warm-up	15	Same as previous workout.
Dynamic Stretching & Form Training .	12-15	Same as previous workout.
Sprint-assisted Training	30	Complete sprinting workout #27 in Table 8.3 using surgical tubing or downhill sprinting.
Speed Endurance Training	20	Complete workout #27 in Table 8.4.
Cool-down	10	Jog 1/2 mile in 6-7 minutes. Walk 1/4 mile in 4 minutes.
Weight Training	45	Early adolescent athletes: Complete workout #27 in Table 8.1.
	60	Adolescent and adult athletes: Complete workout #27 in Table 8.2.
Plyometrics	20	Adolescent and adult athletes: Complete workout #27 in Table 8.5. Early adolescent athletes: Not recommended.

ACTIVITY	TIME (MIN)	SPECIFIC ACTIVITY
Static Stretching	10-12	Same as previous workout.

WORKOUT # 28

Warm-up	15	Same as previous workout.
Dynamic Stretching & Form Training .	12-15	Same as previous workout.
Sprint-assisted Training	30	Repeat the cycling workout you completed in workout #26.
Speed Endurance Training	20	Complete workout #28 in Table 8.4.
Cool-down	10	Jog 1/2 mile in 6-7 minutes. Walk 1/4 mile in 4 minutes.
Weight Training	60	Adolescent and adult athletes: Complete workout #28 in Table 8.2.
Plyometrics	20	Adolescent and adult athletes: Complete workout #28 in Table 8.5. Early adolescent athletes: Not recommended.
Static Stretching	10-12	Same as previous workout.

WORKOUT # 29

Warm-up	15	Same as previous workout.
Dynamic Stretching & Form Training .	12-15	Same as previous workout.

ACTIVITY	TIME (MIN)	SPECIFIC ACTIVITY
Sprint-assisted Training	40	Complete workout # 29 in table 8.3
Speed Endurance Training	20	Complete workout #29 in Table 8.4.
Cool-down	10	Jog 1/2 mile in 6-7 minutes. Walk 1/4 mile in 4 minutes.
Weight Training	45	Early adolescent athletes: Complete workout #29 in Table 8.1.
	60	Adolescent and adult athletes: Complete workout #29 in Table 8.2.
Static Stretching	10-12	Same as previous workout.

WORKOUT # 30   PRACTICE MAINTENANCE PROGRAM

Maintenance Program		Use the workout described below at least once weekly to maintain the gains you have acquired. If you notice a loss of strength, power or speed endurance, add a second maintenance work out using a Monday-Friday or Tuesday-Saturday schedule.
Warm-up	15	Same as previous workout. Be certain to include practice starts, falling starts and near equal thrust off both feet at take-off.
Dynamic Stretching & Form training	12-15	Same as previous workout.
Final Retest		Return to Chapter 1 and complete the following tests once again. Stationary 120-yard dash, Stride length,

ACTIVITY	TIME (MIN)	SPECIFIC ACTIVITY
		Speed Endurance, Leg Strength, Hamstring/Quadriceps Strength. Compare your scores to both the pre-test and mid-test results.
Sprint-Assisted Training	20	Complete maintenance workout #30 in Table 8.3.
Sprint Loading	15	Complete Maintenance workout #30 in Table 8.6.
Cool-down	10	Jog 1/2 mile in 6-7 minutes. Walk 1/4 mile in 4 minutes.
Weight Training	40	Early adolescent athletes: Complete workout #30 in Table 8.1.
	50	Adolescent and adult athletes: Complete workout #30 in Table 8.2.
Plyometrics	15	Adolescent and adult athletes: Complete workout #30 in Table 8.5. Early adolescent athletes: Not recommended.
Speed Endurance Training	20	Complete workout #30 in Table 8.4.
Static Stretching	10-12	Complete each exercise one time, using the Developmental stretch method and a 60 second hold

Table 8.1 Weight Training Program for Early Adolescent Athletes

Exercise	Repetitions	Sets	Rest	Weight
Workouts# 1 and #3 - Concentrate on learning the correct form for each exercise. Use a spotter and do each repetition correctly. Two workouts weekly.				
Foundation Program:				
Leg/back				
Leg Press	12	1	2 Min. between each exercise.	Amount of wt. that allows you to do 12 repetitions with only slight difficulty finishing the final two. Light weight allows you to concentrate on doing quality repetitions with perfect form.
Leg Extensions	12	1		
Leg Curl	12	1		
Seated Row	12	1		
Shoulders/arms				
Lat pull-down	12	1		
Bench press	12	1		
Shoulder Press	12	1		
Triceps Extension	12	1		
Arm Curls 12		1		
Trunk/abdomen:				
Reverse Curl	15	1		
Oblique Twister	15	1		
Crunch	15	1		
Workouts #4 and #6 (Same exercises as above)	13	1	Same	Add one repetition, 2-5 to each trunk/ abdominal exercise.
Workouts #7 and #9 (Same basic exercises)	13	1	Same	Same as above
Workouts #10 and #12 (Same basic exercises)	14	1	Same	Same as above
Workouts #13 and #15	15	1	Same	Same as above

Exercise	Repetitions	Sets	Rest	Weight
(Same basic exercises) **Workouts #16 and #18**	12	2	1 Min. between each exercise, 2 between sets	Return to 12 repetitions, add 5 ib. to upper body & to lower body exercises, 2-5 to trunk/abdominal exercises.
(Same basic exercises) Replace trunk/abdomen exercises with: Knee Tucks, Twisting Crunches & Gravity fighters				
Workouts # 20 and #22 (Same Basic Exercises)	13	2	Same	Same as above
Add sprinter's exercises: Sprint-arm (dumbbells)	12	1		Same as above
Pull-down (single leg)	12	1		
Kick back (single leg)	12	1		
Knee Rise (single leg)	12	1		
Workouts #23 and #25 (Same Basic Exercises)	14	2	Same	Same as above
Sprinter's Exercises	13	1	Same	Same as above
Workouts #27 and #29 (Same Basic Exercises)	15	2	Same	Same as above
Sprinter's Exercises	14	1	Same	Same as above

Workout #30 - Maintenance Program: If an In-season weight training program is provided or by your coach or trainer, follow that program. If not, complete the following workout once weekly in the middle of the week.

Exercise	Repetitions	Sets	Rest	Weight
Same Basic Exercises	10-12	2	1 Min. between	Weight that allows you to do 10 repetitions.
Sprinter's Exercises	10-12	2		

Table 8.2 Weight Training Program for Late Adolescent and Adult Athletes

- Consult your coach, physical education instructor, or weight room expert to help you learn the correct technique (form) for each weight training exercise.
- Avoid sacrificing form for repetitions. Do each exercise correctly.
- See Appendix for a description and drawing of each abdominal exercise.

Micro cycle 1: Preconditioning Cycle   **(3 weeks)**

Exercise	Repeti-tions	Sets	Rest	Weight

WORKOUT # 1, 2, & 3 - Concentrate on learning the correct form for each exercise. Use a spotter at all times. Complete two workouts per week.

Foundation Program:

Exercise	Repeti-tions	Sets	Rest	Weight
Leg/back				
Leg Press	6-9	1	1 minute	Amount of wt. that allows you to do only 9 repetitions. Add 1-2 repetitions each workout, 2-5 for trunk/ abdominal exercises.
Leg extensions 6-9	1			
Leg Curls	6-9	1	each	
Heel Raises	6-9	1	exercise	
Front Squat Lunge	6-9	1		
Shoulders/arms				
Bent-arm fly6-9	1	1		When you can complete 2 or more repetitions above the intended number on two con- secutive workouts, add 5 lb. to arm and add 10 lbs. to leg exercises.
Bench Press	6-9	1		
Standing Triceps	6-9			
Arm Curls 6-9	1			
Military press	6-9	1		
Trunk/abdomen:				

Exercise	Repetitions	Sets	Rest	Weight
Reverse Curl	15-20			
Oblique Twister	15-20	1		
Crunch	15-20	1		

WORKOUT #4, 5 & 6
(Same Basic Exercises)

Exercise	Repetitions	Sets	Rest	Weight
Trunk/abdomen:	6-9	2	Same	Follow the same progression above.
	20-25	1	Same	

WORKOUT #7, 8 and 9
(Same Basic Exercises)

Exercise	Repetitions	Sets	Rest	Weight
Trunk/abdomen:	6-9	2	Same	Follow the same progression above.
	25-30	1	Same	

Micro Cycle 2: Speed-Strength Cycle (3 weeks) Before you begin this cycle, find your 1 RM (maximum weight you can lift 1 time) for each weight training exercise. Your correct weight will be the percentage of that maximum lift shown in the right hand column.

WORKOUT #10, #11, and #12 Add 1 repetition per set in # 11 and #12
(Same Basic Exercises)

Exercise	Repetitions	Sets	Rest	Weight
	1-3	2	2 Min. between sets	75% of maximum lift.
	3-5	2		70% of maximum lift
	5-7	2		60% of maximum lift
Olympic Lifts: Clean, Jerk, Snatch	1-3	2	4 Min.	60% of 1RM
Trunk/abdomen:	30-35	2	Same	

WORKOUT # 13, #14, and #15 Add 1 repetition per set in workouts **#14 and #15**
(Same Basic Exercises)

Exercise	Repetitions	Sets	Rest	Weight
	1-3	2	2 Min.	80% of maximum lift
	3-5	2		75% of maximum lift.
	5-7	2		65% of maximum lift

Table 8.2 Weight Training Program for Late Adolescent and Adult Athletes (continued)

Exercise	Repetitions	Sets	Rest	Weight
Olympic Lifts	1-3	2	4 Min.	65% of maximum lift
Trunk/abdomen:	30-35	1	Same	
WORKOUT #16, #17, and #18 Add 1 repetition per set in workouts #17 and #18				
(Same Basic Exercises)	1-3	3	2 Min.	
	3-5	3		85% of maximum lift
	5-7	3		80% of maximum lift.
	8-15	3		70% of maximum lift
Olympic Lifts	3-5	3		60% of maximum lift
Trunk/abdomen:	30-35	2	3 1/2 Min.	70% of maximum lift
Knee Tucks				Same
Twisting Crunches				
Gravity Fighters				

Micro Cycle 3: Speed Specific Cycle   (2 Weeks)

WORKOUT #19, #20, and #21 Add 1 repetition per set in workouts #20 and #21
Complete two sets of each % of your maximum per exercise.

Exercise	Repetitions	Sets	Rest	Weight
(Group II Exercises)	1-3		2 min.	85% of maximum lift
Incline bench press, dead	3-5		2 min.	80% of maximum lift.
lift, barbell row, shoulder	5-7		2 min.	70% of maximum lift
shrug, bent-over lateral	8-15		2 min.	60% of maximum lift
reverse curl, wrist				
curl, one dumbbell heel raise				

Exercise	Repetitions	Sets	Rest	Weight
Sprinter's exercises:				
Sprint-arm/Paw-down/	1-3	1		75% of maximum lift
	3-5	1		65% of maximum lift
Olympic Lifts	3-5	3	3 1/2 Min.	80% of maximum lift
Trunk/abdomen:	30-35	1	Same	

WORKOUT #22, #23, and #24 Start with the % of maximum lift. Do as many repetitions as you can, remove 5 lb. of weight on upper body and 10 lb. of weight on lower body exercises and complete a second set. For the sprinter's exercises, add 1-2 repetitions in workouts #23 and #24.

Exercise	Repetitions	Sets	Rest	Weight
Same Group II Exercises	Max.	2	2 Min.	85% of maximum lift
	Max.	2		80% of maximum lift
	Max.	2		70% of maximum lift
	Max	1		60% of maximum lift
Sprinter's exercises:				
Sprint-arm/Paw-down/	1-3	1		80% of maximum lift
Kick back/Knee rise	3-5	1		75% of maximum lift
	5-7	1		70% of maximum lift
	8-15	1		60% of maximum lift
Olympic Lifts	3-5	4	3 Min.	80% of maximum lift
Trunk/abdomen:	30-35	1	Same	

Micro Cycle 4: High Intensity Speed-Specific Cycle (2 Weeks: 6 workouts)

WORKOUT #25, 26 & 27 Find your 1 RM (maximum lift weight) for each exercise once again. Complete the workout using the new percentages. Add one or more repetition to each exercise in workouts # 26 and #27

Exercise	Repetitions	Sets	Rest	Weight
Same Group II Exercises	1-3	2	2 Min.	80% of maximum lift
	3-5	2		75% of maximum lift
	5-7	2		70% of maximum lift
	8-15	2		60% of maximum lift

Table 8.2 Weight Training Program for Late Adolescent and Adult Athletes (continued)

Exercise	Repetitions	Sets	Rest	Weight
Sprinter's exercises:				
Sprint-arm/Paw-down/	1-3	2	2 Min.	80% of maximum lift
	3-5	2		75% of maximum lift
Kick back/Knee rise	5-7	2		70% of maximum lift
	8-15	2		60% of maximum lift
Olympic Lifts	3-5	5	2 1/2 Min.	85% of maximum lift
Trunk/abdomen	45	2		

WORKOUT #28 and #29 Complete three sets of each exercise.

Exercise	Repetitions	Sets	Rest	Weight
Same Group II Exercises	2	3	2 Min.	80% of maximum lift
	4	3		75% of maximum lift
	6	3		70% of maximum lift
	10	3		60% of maximum lift
Sprinter's exercises:				
Sprint-arm/Paw-down/	2	3	2 Min.	80% of maximum lift
	4	3		75% of maximum lift
Kick back/Knee rise	6	3		70% of maximum lift
	10	3		60% of maximum lift
Olympic Lifts	3-5	6	2 Min.	90% of maximum lift
Trunk/abdomen	45	2		

WORKOUT #30 - Maintenance Program:

If an In-season weight training program is provided or recommended by your coach or trainer, follow that program. If not, complete the following workout once weekly in the middle of the week. Find your new 1RM for each exercise at least once every 3-4 weeks.

Exercise	Repetitions	Sets	Rest	Weight
(Same Group II Exercises)	1-3	2	2 Min.	80% of maximum

Exercise	Repetitions	Sets	Rest	Weight
Sprinter's exercises:				
Sprint-arm/Paw-down/	3-5	2		75% of maximum
	5-7	2		70% of maximum
	8-15	2		60% of maximum
Kick back/Knee rise	1-3	2	2 Min.	80% of maximum
	3-5	2		75% of maximum
	5-7	2		70% of maximum
	8-15	2		60% of maximum
Olympic Lifts	3-5	3	2 Min.	75% of maximum
Trunk/abdomen	45	2		

Objective	1RM (%)			Speed of each Explosive
Maximum Strength	75-100			Explosive
Speed Strength	60-85			Explosive/Maximal
Strength Endurance	40-60			Explosive

Table 8.3 Sprint-assisted Training - Towing with Surgical Tubing and Downhill Sprinting

Begins in Cycle 2: Speed-Strength Cycle - These first three workouts will help you adjust to the use of surgical tubing and the pulling action as you maintain proper sprinting form at all times. Do not exceed a 3/4 speed striding action in any of the workouts. The Sprint-assisted distance represents the distance towed or the actual downhill distance covered and does not include the 20-25 yard distance used to accelerate to maximum speed or the final 10-meters you should sprint without assistance at the end of each repetition. For ideal downhill sprinting, a 20-25-yard flat surface area (used to accelerate to near maximum speed) is followed by a 15-30 yard downhill area with a one to two and one-half degree slope (to force higher than normal stride rates and speed) and ends with another flat area of 20-25 yards (to allow you to try to hold the higher speeds on your own).

Early adolescent athletes should reduce each workout (repetitions and sets) by 30-50%.

Week/Workout		Overspeed distance	Repetitions	Rest Interval
6	16	1/2 speed runs toward the pull for 15 yards emphasizing correct sprinting form.	5	1 Min.
		1/2 speed backward runs toward the pull for 15 yards.	3	1 Min.
6	17	3/4 speed runs for 20 yards with perfect sprinting form.	5	2 Min.
		3/4 speed backward runs toward the pull for 20 yards	3	2 Min.
6	18	3/4 speed runs for 25 yards.	5	2 Min.
		3/4 backward runs toward the pull for 25 yards.	3	2 Min
		3/4 speed turn-and-runs at a 45 degree angle for 25 yards (right and left)	3	2 Min.

Cycle 3: Speed-Specific Cycle - Two workouts weekly on Monday and Friday or Tuesday and Saturday. Due to the assisted action of the pull, you will now be sprinting at sub-maximum speed in each workout. Although the preconditioning period has prepared you for this training, you can expect to experience muscle soreness the first 5-7 days of sprint-assisted training. Your distances covered should reflect the average distance sprinted in your sport. See the chart at the bottom of the table. Keep in mind that Sprint-assisted Training is NOT a conditioning activity and full recovery between each repetition is important.

Week/Workout	Overspeed distance	Repetitions	Rest Interval
7 19	3/4 speed runs toward the pull for 15 yards.	3	2 Min.
	Maximum sprinting speed toward the pull for 15 yards	5	2 Min.
7 21	3/4 speed runs for 20 yards.	3	2 Min
	Maximum speed for 20 yards	6	2 1/2 Min.
8 22	3/4 speed runs for 25 yards	3	2 Min.
	Maximum speed sprints for 25 yards	6	3 Min.
8 24	3/4 speed sprints for 30 yards	3	2 Min.
	Maximum speed sprints for 30 yards	6	3 Min.

Cycle 4: High Intensity Speed-Specific Cycle - The emphasis in this cycle is on fast leg and arm turn-over in each exercise.

Week/Workout	Overspeed distance	Repetitions	Rest Interval
9 25	3/4 speed runs toward the pull for 15 yards.	3	1 Min.
	Quick feet, short step, low knee lift sprint for 15 yards with rapid arm pumping action.	3	2 Min.
	Quick feet, short step, fast high knee lift sprint for 15 yards with rapid arm pumping action.	3	2 Min.
	Maximum speed pulls for 30 yards.	4	3 Min.
9 26	High speed stationary cycling. With the resistance on low-to-average, warm-up for 5-7 min. until you perspire freely. Pedal at 3/4 speed for 30 seconds	3	1 Min
	Pedal at maximum speed for 2 seconds as you say"one thousand and one, one thousand and two say"one thousand and one, one thousand and two Repeat above for 3 seconds.	7	2 Min.
	Maximum speed for 20 yards	3	2 Min.
	Repeat workout #25	6	2 1/2 Min.
9 27	Add two-man pull-and-resist drill for 100 yards.	2	4 Min.
	Maximum speed sprints for 25 yards	6	3 Min.

1Table 8.3 Sprint-assisted Training - Towing with Surgical Tubing and Downhill Sprinting (con't)

Week/Workout	Overspeed distance	Repetitions	Rest Interval
10 28	Repeat stationary cycling workout # 26	3	
10 29	3/4 speed runs toward the pull for 15 yards.	3	1 Min.
	Quick feet, short step, low knee lift sprint for 15 yards with rapid arm pumping action.	5	2 Min.
	Quick feet, short step, high knee life sprint for 15 yards with rapid arm pumping action.	5	2 Min.
	Maximum speed pulls for 30 yards.	5	3 Min.
	MAINTENANCE PROGRAM		
10 30	3/4 speed runs toward the pull for 15 yards	2	2 Min.
	Quick feet, short step, high knee life sprint for 15 yards with rapid arm pumping action.	2	2 Min.
	Maximum speed pull forward for 20 yards, plant right foot and sprint diagonally left for 20 yards. Repeat planting the left foot and sprinting diagonally right for 20 yards.	3	2 Min
	Maximum speed pulls forward for 30 yards	3	2 Min

Sport	Distance Sprinted	Rest between sprin
Baseball, Softball	30 yards	Use 30-60 seconds.
Basketball	30 yards	5-30 seconds
Football	25 yards	25-30 seconds (huddle time)
Soccer, Lacrosse, & Rugby	40 yards	Continuous play, 5-15 seconds
Tennis	10 yards	3-5 seconds in same point, 20-30 seconds between points, 60 seconds between games
Handball, Racquetball, Squash	3-5 yards	5-10 seconds between points.

Table 8.4 Speed Endurance Training

Begins in Cycle 2: Speed-Strength Cycle - Early adolescent athletes should reduce the number of repetitions in each workout by 50%.

Week/Workout		Routine/Distance	Repetitions	Rest Interval
3	7	Jog 15 yards, stride 15 (3/4 speed), jog 15, walk 15	3	No rest between repetitions; the walk is the recovery phase.
3	9	Same as previous workout	4	Same
4	10	Same as previous workout	5	Same
4	12	Jog 15 yards, stride 15 (3/4 speed), sprint 15, walk 15	4	Same
5	13	Same as previous workout	5	Same.
5	15	Same as previous workout	6	Same
6	16	Jog 25 yards, stride 25 (3/4 speed), sprint 25, walk 25	4	Same
6	18	Same as previous workout	5	Same

Cycle 3: Speed-Specific Cycle - The increases in the distance each repetition represents over-distance training and may be more than the typical distance you sprint in your sport.

Week/Workout		Routine/Distance	Repetitions	Rest Interval
7	19	Sprint 40 yards	6	Walk 30 seconds
		300-meter sprint	1	

Table 8.4 Speed Endurance Training   **(continued)**

Week/Workout	Routine/Distance	Repetitions	Rest Interval
7 21	Same as previous workout	8	Same
8 22	Sprint 60 yards	6	Same
	300-meter sprint	2	3 Min.
8 24	Same as previous workout	8	Same

Cycle 4: High Intensity Speed-Specific Cycle - The distance covered reflects the average distance you sprint during competition in your sport. The rest interval between each sprint should be equal to the amount of rest that occurs between sprints during competition.

Week/Workout	Routine/Distance	Repetitions	Rest Interval
9 25	Sprint 75 yards	8	25 seconds
	300 yard sprint	2	3 Min.
9 26	Sprint 75 yards	10	20 seconds
	300 yard sprint	3	2 1/2 Min.
9 27	Sprint 75 yards	12	15 seconds
	300 yard sprint	2	2 1/2 Min.
	Sprinting in place with high knee lift to exhaustion	1	
10 28	300 meter sprint	3	2 minutes

Week/Workout	Routine/Distance	Repetitions	Rest Interval
10 29	300 meter sprint	4	2 minutes
10 30	MAINTENANCE WORKOUT - based on average distance sprinted in various sports shown below. Sprint 5 repetitions at the distance specified for your sport. the number of seconds indicated in the right-hand column between each repetition and end the workout with two 300-meter sprints using a two minute rest period between repetitions.		

Sport	Distance Sprinted	Rest between sprints
Baseball, Softball	30 yards	Use 30-60 seconds.
Basketball	30 yards	5-30 seconds
Football	25 yards	25-30 seconds (huddle time)
Soccer, Lacrosse, Rugby	40 yards	Continuous play, 5-15 seconds
Tennis 10 yards		3-5 seconds in same point, yards 20-30 seconds between points, 60 seconds between games
Handball, racquetball, squash	3-5 yards	5-10 seconds between points.

Table 8.5 Plyometrics

Begins in Cycle 2: Speed-Strength Cycle - This three week cycle emphasizes speed- strength and moves into plyometrics, sprint-assisted training, and speed endurance training as your program develops into a near complete speed improvement program. Plyometric workouts should not exceed 80-100 jumps, leaps, and bounds per session for beginners and athletes in early workouts, 100-120 per session for intermediates and 120-140 for athletes who have had 4-6 weeks of plyometric training. The emphasis is on quality jumps and form, rather than volume. Polymetric training is not recommended for preadolescent and early adolescent athletes.

Week/Workout	Routine/Distance	Repetitions	Sets	Rest Interval
4	11	Low Intensity Program: Master the correct form for each exercise.			
		Squat jump	4	2	2 Min. between sets
		Double-leg ankle bounce	4	2	2 Min.
		Lateral cone jump	4	2	2 Min.
		Drop and catch push-up	4	2	2 Min.
		Lateral cone jump	4	2	2 Min.
		Standing triple jump	4	2	2 Min.
		Double leg tuck	4	2	2 Min.
4	12	Same as previous workout.	4	2	2 Min.
5	14	Same as previous workout.	5	2	2 Min.
5	17	Same as previous workout.	6	2	2 Min.
6	20	Medium Intensity:			
		Standing long jump	6	2	2 Min

Week/Workout		Routine/Distance	Repetitions	Sets	Rest Interval
8	22	Alternate-leg bound	6	2	2 Min
		Double-leg hop	6	2	2 Min
		Pike jump	6	2	2 Min
		Depth jumps	6	2	2 Min
		Dumbbell arm swings	6	2	2 Min
8	23	Same as previous workout	7	2	2 Min.
9	26	Same as previous workout	8	2	2 Min.
		High Intensity:			
		Single-leg vertical power jump	6	2	90 Seconds
		Single-leg speed hop	6	2	90 Seconds
		Double-leg speed hop	6	2	90 Seconds
		Multiple box jumps	6	2	90 Seconds
		Side jump and sprint	6	2	90 Seconds
		Decline hops	6	2	90 Seconds
		Sprint arm action	6	2	90 Seconds
		Medicine ball sit-up	7	2	90 seconds
9	27	Same as previous workout	8	2	90 seconds
10	28	Same as previous workout	8	2	90 Seconds
10	30	Same as previous workout			

Table 8.6 Sprint Loading Program: Hill Sprinting, Stadium Stairs, Weighted Vests or Sled

Week/Workout		Routine/Distance	Repetitions	Sets	Rest Interval
Cycle 1: Preconditioning and Acclimation Cycle					
2	6	1/2 speed Power Starts in uphill sprinting or Sled with no weight for 15 yards.*	3	1	Walk back to the starting position.
3	7	Repeat above at 3/4 speed.	3	1	Same
3	9	Repeat the previous workout.	3	2	Same
4	11	Repeat the previous workout.	4	2	Same
		Repeat the previous workout. Add weight to sled or vests and accelerate to maximum speed and hold for 15 yards.	5	2	Same
Cycle 2: Speed-Strength Cycle (3 Weeks)					
5	13	Repeat previous workout accelerating for 25 yards.	5	2	Same
5	15	Same as previous workout. Add weight to sled or vest.	5	2	Same
6	17	Repeat previous workout accelerating for 30 yards	4	2	Same

Week/Workout		Routine/Distance	Repetitions	Sets	Rest Interval
Cycle 3: Speed Specific (2 Weeks)					
7	19	Remove weight from Sled/vest and return to a slightly reduced incline. Accelerate at maximum speed and sprint 40 yards.		3	Same
8	21	Repeat previous workout. Finish with one all-out 100-yd. acceleration sprint.	5	3	Same
8	23	Repeat above workout	5	3	Same
Cycle 4: High Intensity Speed-Specific Cycle - Sprint Loading is not included in this two-week cycle.					
10	30	Maintenance load. Remove weight from Sled/vest or use no more than a 3% incline. Accelerate to maximum speed and sprint 40 yds.	4	3	Same

Actual distance you are pulling the sled, sprinting with weighted vests, or sprinting uphill or up stadium steps.

APPENDIX A: YOUR TEST SCORE SHEET

Name _____   Age ____ Height ____ Weight ____
Sport _____   Starting Date _____

Test Item	Score	Standard	Weakness*
General Speed Tests:			
Stationary 120-yd dash		Everyone can improve their	Scores are used to find weakness areas below.
40-yd. time		40-yd, Flying 40-yard and	X Yes
Flying 40-yd. time		120-yard time.	
Strength and Power Tests:			
Leg Strength-Double-leg press		Multiply your body weight X 2.5. Your leg press score should be higher.	___ Yes ___ No
Two Leg Curl (quadriceps) L ___ R ___		Leg curl scores should be at least 80% of leg extension scores. Do each leg separately. Right and	___ Yes ___ No
Leg Extension (quadriceps) L ___ R ___		left leg scores in both areas should be almost the same (within 5-10%).	___ Yes ___ No

Test Item	Score		Standard	Weakness*
Standing Triple Jump			Males: at least 20' (middle school), 25' (H.S.), 28' (college); Females: 15' (middle school), 20' (H.S.), 23' (college)	___Yes ___No
Power Kick-back	L ___ R ___		If the difference between the right and left leg scores exceed five pounds, a muscle imbalance exists.	___Yes ___No
Difference Quick Feet	___ ___		Males: at least 3.8 (middle school), 4.2 (middle school), 3.3 (H.S.) and 2.8 (college). Females: 4.2 (middle	___Yes ___No
1. Stride Rate	___		With your stride length and flying 40 scores, find your stride rate using the formula in Chapter 3. Since everyone can improve their stride rate, yes is checked.	X Yes ___
2. Stride Length	___ ___		Scores should be within these ranges: Males: 1.14 X height + or - 4 inches Females: 1.15 X height or 2.16 X leg length.	___Yes ___No

APPENDIX A: YOUR TEST SCORE SHEET (continued)

est Item	Score	Standard	Weakness*
Right leg push-off score Left leg push-off score Difference	‖ ‖ ‖	If the difference in the right and left leg exceed 2-3", a muscle imbalance is suggested.	__Yes __Yes
3. Start & Acceleration Flying 40-yd. time minus Stationary 40-yd time	‖	No more than 7/10 difference between the Flying 40 and your your Stationary 40-yd time	__Yes __No
4. Form Errors	‖	List the form errors found from slow-motion analysis of video taped 40-yd. dash or coach observation.	__Yes __No
5. Speed Endurance Flying 40-yd. time minus your 80-120-yd time	‖	No more than 2/10 second difference between flying 40 and 80-120	__Yes __No

Each of the test areas are listed in the left-hand column below. If your scores in any of these areas did not meet the minimum standard, check (√) the training program in the right-hand column that you need to follow to eliminate the weakness.

Areas	Training Programs	
1. Stride Rate	√ Sprint-assisted	√ Strength Training
2. Stride Length	_ Sprint-assisted	_ Strength Training
	_ Plyometrics	
3. Start and Acceleration	_ Sprint loading	_ Plyometrics
	_ Sprint-Assisted Training	
	_ Form Training	_ Strength training
4. Form	_ Form Training	
5. Speed Endurance	_ Speed endurance training	
	_ Speed Strength training	

Now, do the same for your scores in each of the General Strength Tests:

Test	Training Programs	
Leg Strength (two-leg press)	_ Strength training	_ Plyometric Training
L & R Leg Curl	_ Strength training	_ Plyometric Training
L & R leg Extension	_ Strength training	_ Plyometric Training
L & R Power Kick-back	_ Strength training	_ Plyometric Training

APPENDIX B: SPEED EMPHASIS AREAS FOR VARIOUS SPORTS

Sport	Emphasis areas by Priority	Comment
Soccer field hockey, ice hockey lacrosse rugby	1. Acceleration: starting ability 2. Speed: stride rate, stride length 3. Speed endurance	In the open field, sprinting faster occurs only by taking faster or longer steps. Speed endurance is important only to prevent slowing after repeated sprints.
Basketball, tennis	1. Acceleration: starting ability 2. Speed: stride rate, 3. Speed endurance 4. Stride length	Most explosive action occurs after some slight movement has taken place (a jog, a bounce, a side ward step). Maximum speed is never reached.
Baseball	1. Acceleration: starting ability 2. Speed: stride rate, stride length 3. Speed endurance	Players rarely approach maximum speed unless a triple or inside-the-park home run occurs. Starting ability and acceleration are most important.

Sport	Emphasis areas by Priority	Comment
Football	1. Acceleration: Starting ability 2. Speed: stride rate 3. Speed endurance 4. Stride length	Acceleration from a three or four-pt. stance or standing position is critical to every player. Stride rate and length determine mph speed in the open field. Speed endurance prevents slowing at the end of a long run or after repeated sprints due to fatigue.
Track (100m)	1. Acceleration: starting ability 2. Speed: stride rate,	A 100m- or 200m dash sprinter must work in all areas in near equal pro-portion. The start and acceleration are more critical in the 100m race

APPENDIX C:

LOWER AND UPPER ABDOMINAL EXERCISES

Reverse Curls

Lie on the floor with fingers locked behind your head. Knees are bent. Contract your lower abs to curl hips off the ground about 3 - 5 inches bringing knees towards chest. Slowly return to the floor. Do not "whip" your legs. Let the abs do the work. Remember to press your lower back into floor throughout the exercise.

Knee Tucks

Lie on your back with hands supporting your head. Tuck one knee to your chest and extend the other straight a few inches off the floor. Hold 2 counts and switch legs. Some hip flexor work is involved, but keeping the low back pressed to the floor will work the lower abs isometrically.

Oblique Twisters

Lie on your back, bend your knees, and point both knees to the left. Extend your arms over your right hip. Slowly curl shoulders and upper back off the floor to a half-upright position. Reverse the curl to return to the floor. Repeat with the opposite side.

Twisting Crunches

Lie on your back with knees bent, ankles crossed and fixed. Contract abdominals to lift shoulder and upper back off floor. Twist trunk, bringing left elbow to right knee. Repeat to opposite side.

Crunches

Lie on your back with knees bent, feet flat on the floor. Hands support your head. Look at the ceiling and contract the abs to lift the shoulders and upper back off the floor. Lift one knee and bring it in toward your elbow. Press the low back to the floor, hold briefly, then return to floor.

Gravity fighters

Start with knees bent, feet flat and body rounded to a position 45 degrees off the floor. Arms are crossed over the chest, chin is tucked. The body is gradually lowered until the shoulder blades touch the floor. Reverse the movement to starting position.

SUGGESTED READING
AND VIEWING

Allerheligen, W.B. 1994. Speed development and plyometric training. In T.R. Baechle (Ed). *Essentials of strength training and conditioning* (pp. 314-344). Champaign, IL: Human Kinetics

Alter, Michael J. 1998. *Sport Stretch.* Champaign, IL.: Human Kinetics.

Baechle, T., Ed. 1994. *Essentials of Strength Training and Conditioning.* Champaign, IL.: Human Kinetics.

Baker, D. Selecting the appropriate exercises and loads for speed-strength development. *Strength and Conditioning Coach* 3 (2: 8-16): 1995.

Bell, Sam., 2000. Drills which lead to better sprint performance. In *Sprint and Relays: Contemporary Theory,* Technique and Training. 5th Ed., Mountain View, CA: Tafnews Press, p-91

Bompa, Tudor, and Cornacchia, Lorenzo, 1999. *Serious Strength Training: Periodization for Building Muscle Power and Mass* . Champaign, Ill.: Human Kinetics

Chu, D. 1998. *Jumping Into Plyometrics.* Champaign, IL: Human Kinetics.

Chui, Donald A., 1999. *Explosive Power and Strength.* Champaign, Ill.: Human Kinetics.

Delecluse, C., Influence of strength training on sprint running performance: Current findings and implications for training. *Sports Medicine* 24(3): 147-156: 1997.

Delecluse, C., Van Coppenolle H., Goris M.; Diels, R. Analysis of the front and rear foot action in the sprint start.

In Bruggemann, G.P., and Ruhl,   J.K. (Eds) *Techniques in Athletics Conference Proceedings.* Volume 2, pp. 402-406: 1990.

Dintiman, George B., and Ward, Robert, 2003. *Sportspeed III.* Champaign, IL.: Human Kinetics.

Dintiman, George B. (1987) Speed Improvement for Football. *Sportspeed Magazine* Vol 2, October (published by the National Association of Speed and Explosion, Box 1784, Kill Devil Hills, NC 27948)

Dintiman, George B., 1980. The effects of high-speed treadmill training upon stride length, stride rate, and sprinting speed.Unpublished Work. Virginia Commonwealth University.

Dintiman, George B., 1974. *What Research Tells the Coach about Sprinting.* AAHPERD, Reston, VA.

Dintiman, George., 1970. *Sprinting Speed: Its Improvement for Major Sports Competition.* Springfield, Illinois: Charles C. Thomas, Publishers.

Dintiman, G. The relationship between the leg strength/body weight ratio and running speed. *The Bulletin of the Connecticut Association for Health, Physical Education, and Recreation* 11:5: 1966.

Dintiman, George B., The effects of various training programs on running speed. *Research Quarterly.* 35: 456-63: 1964.

Dowson M. N., Nevill M. E., Lakomy H. K., Nevill A. M. and Hazeldine R. J. Modeling the relationship between isokinetic muscle strength and sprint running performance. *J Sports Sci* 16: 257-265, 1998.

Figoni, S., C.B. Christ, and B.H. Mossey. Effects of speed, hip, knee angle, and gravity on hamstring to quadriceps torque ratios. *Journal of Orthopedics Sports and Physical Therapy* 9(8):287-291: 1988.

Foran, Bill (Ed.) 2001. *High Performance Sports Training.* Champaign, Ill.: Human Kinetics Publishers.

Grace, T., E.R. Sweetser, M.A. Nelson, L.R. Ydens, and B.J. Skipper. Isokinetic muscle imbalance and knee joint injuries. *Journal of Bone and Joint Surgery* 66A:734: 1984.

Herman, D. 1976. The effects of depth jumping on vertical jumping and sprinting speed. Unpublished master's thesis. Ithaca, NY: Ithaca College.

Inglis, Robert, 2000. Training for acceleration in the 100m sprint. *Sprint and Relays: Contemporary Theory, Technique and Training.* 5th Ed., Mountain View, CA: Tafnews Press, pgs. 35-39.

Jakalski, Ken, 2000. Parachutes, Tubing and Towing. *Sprint and Relays:Contemporary Theory, Technique and Training.* 5th Ed., Mountain View, CA: Tafnews Press, pgs. 95-100.

Klinzing, J. Improving sprint speed for all athletes. *NSCA Journal* 6(4):32-33:1984.

Korchemny, R. Evaluation of sprinters. *NSCA Journal* 7(4):38-42: 1985.

Kozlov, V. Muravyev, Muscles and the Sprint. *Fitness and Sports review International* (Vol. 27, #8, 192-195: 1992.

Kraemer, William, and Fleck, Steven, 1993. *Strength Training for Young   Athletes* Champaign, Ill.: Human Kinetics Publishers.

Laird, D.E. 1981. Comparison of quadriceps to hamstring strength ratios of an intercollegiate soccer team. *Athletic Training* 16:666-667: 1981.

Lopez, Victor, 2000. An approach to strength training for sprinters. *Sprint and Relays: Contemporary Theory, Technique and Training.* 5th Ed., Mountain View, CA: Tafnews Press, pgs. 58-63.

Luhtanen, P., and P.V. Komi. Mechanical factors influencing running speed. In *Biomechanics* VI-B, 23-29: 1978, edited by E. Asmussen and E. Jorgensen. Baltimore: University Park Press.

Mann, R. Speed development. *NSCA Journal* 5(6):12-20, 72-73: 1984.

Mero, A., Komi, P.V., & Gregor, R.J. Biomechanics of sprint running: a review. *Sports Medicine.* 13, 376-392: 1992.

Mero, A. Acceleration in the sprint start. *Track Technique* No 105, pg. 3359-3360: 1988.

Moore, J., and G. Wade. Prevention of anterior cruciate ligament injuries. *NSCA Journal* 11(3):35-40: 1989.

Novacheck TF. The biomechanics of running. *Gait Posture* 7: 77-95, 1998.

Parker, M.G., D. Holt, E. Bauman, M. Drayna, and R.O. Ruhling. Descriptive analysis of bilateral quadriceps and hamstring muscle torque in high school football players. *Medicine and Science in Sports and Exercise* 14:152: 1982.

Pauletto, B. Let's talk training: periodization-peaking. *NSCA Journal* 8(4):30-31: 1986.

Rogers, J. 1967. A study to determine the effect of the weight of football uniforms on speed and agility. Master's thesis. Springfield, IL: Springfield College.

Schlinkman, B. Norms for high school football players derived from Cybex data reduction computer. *Journal of Orthopedics Sports and Physical Therapy* 5:410-412: 1984.

Schmolinsky, G. (Editor). Track and Field: *The East German Textbook of Athletics*. Toronto: Sport Books Publishing, 1993.

Smith, L. Individual differences in strength, reaction latency, mass, and length of limbs and their relation to maximal speed of movement. *Research Quarterly* 32:208-220: 1961.

Spassov, A. Bulgarian training methods. Paper presented at the symposium of the *National Strength and Conditioning Association* in Denver, CO, June: 1989.

Thomas, L. Isokinetic torque levels for adult females: effects of age and body size. *Journal of Orthopedics Sports and Physical Therapy* 6:21-24: 1984.

Verkhoshansky, Y. V. Quickness and velocity in sports movements. New Studiesin Athletics 11(2-3): 29-37, 1996.

Verhoshansky, Yuri, Recommended methods of speed development for elite athletes. *Sprint and Relays: Contemporary Theory, Technique and Training*. 5th Ed., Mountain View, CA: Tafnews Press, pgs. 79-82: 2000.

Ward, P.E., and R.D. Ward. 1991. Encyclopedia of Weight Training. Laguna Hills, CA: QPT.

Ward-Smith AJ. Energy conversion strategies during 100 m sprinting. *J Sports Sci* 19: 701-710, 2001.

Weinberg, R., and D. Gould. 1999. *Foundations of sport and exercise psychology.* Champaign, IL: Human Kinetics.

Weyand PG, Sternlight DB, Bellizzi MJ and Wright S. Faster top running speeds   are achieved with greater ground forces not more rapid leg movements. *J Appl Physiol*

Ward, P.E., and R.D. Ward. 1991. *Encyclopedia of Weight Training.* Laguna   Hills, CA: QPT.

Young W, McLean B and Ardagna J. Relationship between strength qualities and sprinting performance. *J Sports Med Phys Fitness* 35: 13-19, 1995.

Young WB, McDowell MH and Scarlett BJ. Specificity of

sprint and agility training methods. *J Strength Cond Res* 15: 315-319, 2001.

VIDEOS

Speed Improvement for Soccer by Dr. George B. Dintiman and Dr. Larry Isaacs, *National Association of Speed and Explosion*, Box 1784, Kill Devil Hills, NC 27948; 1995. Web site: naseinc.com ($19.95)

Speed and Explosion: by Dr. Bob Ward and Dr. George B. Dintiman, featuring the late Tom Landry and Bob Hayes, and Tony Dorsett, Randy White, Doug Donley, Bill Bates and Brian Baldinger. *National Association of Speed and Explosion*, Box 1784, Kill Devil Hills, NC 27948; 1995. Collector's item - Web site: naseinc.com ($19.95).

MEMBERSHIP IN THE NATIONAL ASSOCIATION OF SPEED AND EXPLOSION (naseinc.com)

JOIN THE NASE NOW by completing the form on the next page or online at naseinc.com to enjoy a membership that includes:

- A bimonthly news bulletin with articles by the leading experts in the world on all aspects of training to improve speed in short sprints for team sport athletes from ages 9-25.

- On-line forum for the exchange of ideas and networking with other coaches, athletes and parents.

- 10% off books, videos overspeed training equipment. and the Self-evaluation Program that analyzes 15 test scores and identifies the factors limiting the speed of individual athletes.

- A prestigious certification program in Speed and Explosion for school, university and age group coaches, strength and conditioning coaches, personal trainers, and senior Physical Education majors.

- Discounts on registration fees for symposiums and clinics.

The **NASE** was founded in 1986, by Dr. George B. Dintiman and Dr. Bob Ward, former conditioning coach for the Dallas Cowboys. The National Headquarters is located on the Outer Banks of North Carolina in Kill Devil Hills near the site of the first flight by the Wright Brothers in 1903. The NASE is involved with all aspects of speed improvement for team and individual sports and provides parents and age group, high school and university athletes and coaches, at each level of competition with the latest research and techniques of training to improve speed in short sprints. NASE President, **Dr. Dintiman,** is one of the world's leading authorities on speed improvement for team sports. Author of 41 books on speed improvement, fitness, nutrition, weight control, and preventive disease his speed improvement techniques and books are in use throughout the world. He and his staff (Strength and Conditioning coaches from UCLA, Univ. of Texas at Austin, Notre Dame, Penn State Univ., Grambling Univ., Clemson, Univ. of South Carolina, Univ. of Oregon, Univ..of Kansas, Univ. of Washington, etc.) have worked with athletes of all ages and consulted in the NFL, NBA, MLB, MLS, and in pro tennis.

NATIONAL ASSOCIATION OF SPEED AND EXPLOSION
Membership Application

Name _____

Institution (If applicable) _____

Mailing Address _____

City _____**State** _____ **Zip** _____

Tel. _____ **Fax** _____ **E-mail** _____

Current Position:

Specific Areas of Interest:

Coaching Involvement (if applicable)

Category:
___ Middle/High School Coach   ___ Age Group Coach
___ University Coach   ___ Strength &
___ Athlete - List sport(s):   Conditioning Coach

Membership - Five issues per year of the NASE News Bulletin; Online Forum for exchange of ideas and networking, 10% discounts on books, speed improvement products, and registration at symposiums and clinics, and a certification program for coaches at all levels with testing sites and dates in over 24 states; and more.

Professional- $39.00,
Student (High School or College Undergraduate)- $29.00

I would like to join the NASE. My $ _____check is enclosed.